MARVEL

ABSOLUTELY EVERYTHING YOU NEED TO KNOW...

Written by

ADAM BRAY
LORRAINE CINK
JOHN SAZAKLIS
SVEN WILSON

CHAPTER ONE
CHARACTERS

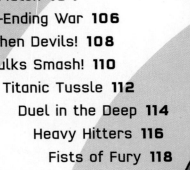

SUPER HEROES 6

"I Can't Surrender" 8

Sentinel of Liberty 10

The Sea King 12

Power Players 14

Iron Man Armours 16

Heavy Metal 18

Pym's Particles 20

Super Sting! 22

Think Small! 24

Hot Shot! 26

God of Thunder 28

Asgard Avenger 30

High Flyer 32

Super Spy 34

Claw of the Jungle 36

Nighttime Ninja 38

Blast Off! 40

"Hulk Smash!" 42

Big Trouble! 44

Hex Power 46

Born to Run 48

"With Great Power…" 50

Webswinger! 52

Spider Science! 54

"Fateful Boon!" 56

Strange Magic 58

Supernatural! 60

Weird and Wonderful 62

SUPER VILLAINS 64

Titan of Terror 66

Mischief Maker! 68

Time-Travelling Tyrant 70

Face of Evil 72

Insane and Loving It! 74

Venomised! 76

Arms Crisis! 78

Dread Lord 80

Barons of Bad 82

Who's the Boss? 84

Magical Menaces 86

Bad Science 88

Lab Rats! 90

If Looks Could Kill 92

Monster Mash 94

CLASSIC CLASHES 96

Temper, Temper! 98

Battling Brothers 100

Power Struggle! 102

Grudge Match 104

Never-Ending War 106

Kitchen Devils! 108

Hulks Smash! 110

Titanic Tussle 112

Duel in the Deep 114

Heavy Hitters 116

Fists of Fury 118

CHAPTER TWO
TEAMS

SUPER HERO TEAMS 122

"Avengers Assemble!" 124

Earth's Mightiest! 126

All Together Now! 128

Mutant Marvels 130

Super Hero Family! 132

The Super Inhumans 134

Troubleshooters! 136

Last Line of Defence 138

Hush-Hush! 140

Fugitives! 142

Squabbles & Superpowers 144

Canada's Champions 146

Looks Aren't Everything! 148

Gods Among Us 150

S.H.I.E.L.D. 152

World Saved! 154

Fast and Furious! 156

Spy Soldiers 158

S.H.I.E.L.D. Operations 160

SUPER VILLAIN TEAMS 162

Many-Headed Menace 164

Troublemakers! 166

Feeling Sinister? 168

Lethal Losers 170

They Come From
Outer Space 172

In the Shadows 174

CONTENTS

CHAPTER THREE
LOCATIONS

Beyond the Stars **178**

The Realm Eternal **180**

"Asgard is No More..." **182**

Mystic Realms **184**

It's a Marvel-ous World! **186**

It's a Jungle Out There! **188**

CHAPTER FOUR
SCIENCE AND MAGIC

MECHANOIDS 192

Rogue Robot **194**

Super Synthezoid **196**

Runaway Bride! **198**

Time for a Change! **200**

More Than Machine **202**

Let's Get Mechanical! **204**

ICONIC ARTEFACTS 206

Liberty's Shield **208**

Hammer of the Gods **210**

Hands Off! **212**

Do You Believe In Magic? **214**

CHAPTER FIVE
KEY EVENTS

WORLD-CHANGING WARS 218

Long Live Doom! **220**

Whose Side Are You On? **222**

This Means War! **224**

Rise of the Robots! **226**

ALTERNATE WORLDS 228

Blast From the Past **230**

Want to Know the Future? **232**

Expect the Unexpected! **234**

INDEX 236

ACKNOWLEDGEMENTS 240

CHAPTER ONE
CHARACTERS

Which villain gives everyone in Manhattan the POWERS OF SPIDER-MAN?

What does Green Goblin ride on to attack Spider-Man before he invents his GOBLIN GLIDER?

How does Hulk FLOOR FOES without even touching them?

SUPER HEROES

"...to make tomorrow's world better. ...always has been... There'll always be *something* to fight for. And I'll *always* be a soldier."

"Reach out. Dare to dream the highest dreams and you will make a difference."

"...to each *and every one of us* to remind ...and anyone who will listen, that *all* ...men and women are created *equal.*"

"I can't surrender. I don't know how!"

"...founded on one principle above all ...we stand up for what we ...or consequences."

"Look into my eyes, tyrant! They're the eyes of a man who would die for liberty!"

9

REALLY?!

While battling **Nightshade**, the "Queen of the Werewolves", Steve Rogers is injected with **yet another serum**. It turns him into a **werewolf!**

NUMBER CRUNCH!

1.87m (6ft 2in)
Steve Rogers' height, post-serum

109kg (240lbs)
Steve Rogers' weight, post-serum

1922
The year Steve Rogers was born

48kph (30mph)
Steve Rogers' max running speed, post-serum

4-F
Steve Rogers' reject classification when he first attempts to enlist in the military

363
The weight in kg Cap can bench-press (800lbs).

Q: Why does Steve Rogers retire as Captain America?

A: When Cap faces the villain Iron Nail, the effects of the Super-Soldier serum are **neutralised** and Rogers **rapidly ages.** Sam Wilson, the Falcon, takes his place as Captain America.

TELL ME MORE!

Scrawny Steve Rogers wants to serve his country and fight the Nazis, but he is rejected for his poor physical condition. When Dr Erskine invites him to join the U.S.A. military's Super-Soldier programme, Operation: Rebirth, he doesn't hesitate!

TOP 5 STAND-IN CAPS

SAM WILSON (FALCON) – takes over when age catches up with Steve Rogers.

BUCKY BARNES (THE WINTER SOLDIER) – best friend Bucky fills in when Cap is seemingly assassinated.

ROSCOE SIMONS – steps in when Cap becomes Nomad – a hero with no nation.

DAVE RICKFORD – a pawn used by Nick Fury to convince Steve Rogers to resume his role.

JOHN WALKER – takes up the role when Rogers resigns, before becoming the U.S. Agent.

S.H.I.E.L.D. DECLASSIFIED

THE WINTER SOLDIER
Bucky Barnes is believed killed when Baron Zemo's airplane explodes at the end of World War II. He returns years later, brainwashed as elite Russian agent the Winter Soldier. Steve Rogers helps his old friend recover his memories.

BETWEEN...

Marvel Comics rebooted World War II hero Captain America in *Avengers* #4 (March 1964). Cap returned with a new backstory – he had been frozen in Arctic ice since 1945!

...THE PANELS

Steve Rogers and Sharon Carter (Agent 13) fall in love but it doesn't work out. She's brainwashed by Dr Faustus to assassinate Cap!

UNLUCKY IN LOVE

BACK FROM THE DEAD!

Cap is apparently assassinated after the superhuman civil war, but he **survives!** He is shot with a special time-travel weapon and has to **relive** major events in his life.

NOOOOO!!

As soon as Steve Rogers receives the Super-Soldier serum, Nazis **KILL** its creator, Dr Erskine. Cap is left as the **ONLY MEMBER** of Operation: Rebirth – started to create an entire **ARMY!**

FAST FACTS

REAL NAME:
Steven Rogers

OCCUPATIONS: Army captain, director of S.H.I.E.L.D., illustrator

MAIN WEAPON: Virtually indestructible shield

STRENGTHS: Slow-aging, inspirational leader, expert fighter, physically perfect, great integrity

WEAKNESSES: His age (when the Super-Soldier serum wears off)

ALLIES: Winter Soldier, Falcon, Nick Fury, Avengers

FOES: Red Skull, Baron Zemo, Hydra, A.I.M.

SENTINEL OF LIBERTY

Captain America is an inspiration to all servicemen in World War II fighting alongside **Nazi villains** and saving the world. Trapped in ice for decades, he is **revived** by the Avengers to **protect and serve**.

THE SEA KING

Namor is the ruler and protector of the underwater kingdom of **Atlantis** and has amazing **aquatic abilities**. Born to **a royal Atlantean mother** and **a human father,** Namor is frequently **at odds** with **"surface-dwellers",** but he fights alongside them when he feels it's in **Atlantis' best interests**.

AAARRGHH!!

Namor is virtually **INVINCIBLE** when in the ocean. Out of water, his **STRENGTH LESSENS,** and after a few days he could even **DIE!**

FAST FACTS

REAL NAME:
Namor McKenzie

NICKNAMES: The Sub-Mariner, The Avenging Son, Imperius Rex

STRENGTHS: Amphibious adaptations to live underwater; superhuman strength, speed, reflexes and durability; flight; extended life-span; telepathy with sea life

WEAKNESSES: Vulnerable to dehydration and pollution; hot-headed

FOES: Attuma, Tiger Shark, Nitro, anyone he thinks threatens Atlantis

REALLY?!

Namor was once **married** to Marinna Smallwood – an **aquatic alien** member of Alpha Flight – until Norman Osborn **mutated** her into an uncontrollable **sea monster!**

ALTERNATE UNIVERSE

In the possible future of **Earth X,** Namor is responsible for the **demise of Johnny Storm** of the Fantastic Four. As penance, Franklin Richards **alters reality** so that one half of Namor's body is **always aflame!**

The **Horn of Proteus** is an Atlantean **artefact** capable of summoning **behemoths** from the deepest depths of the ocean to do the bearer's bidding. Namor has used the Horn to call on such beasts as **Giganto**, an enormous **sperm whale** with **legs and arms**.

S.H.I.E.L.D. DECLASSIFIED

THE INVADERS
Namor fights on the frontlines of World War II against the Axis forces, teaming up with other early heroes as the Invaders. His wartime experiences give Namor a grudging respect for human heroes, especially Captain America (Steve Rogers).

INVISIBLE LOVE
Namor has long carried a torch for Invisible Woman (Sue Richards of the Fantastic Four), but Sue only has eyes for **MISTER FANTASTIC,** her hubby Reed!

"IMPERIUS REX!"
NAMOR'S BATTLE CRY

WOW!

96.6

Namor's top swimming speed in kph (60mph). This is over 13 times quicker than the fastest human swimmer.

WHAT?!

Olympic swimmer Todd Arliss **injures his spine** in a publicity stunt and undergoes an experiment to **mix his DNA** with Namor's and a shark's. He turns into the aquatic, razor-toothed villain **Tiger Shark!**

NOOOOO!!

Possessed by the **PHOENIX FORCE**, Namor demolishes most of the nation of **WAKANDA** with a **TIDAL WAVE!**

WHEN GOOD GUYS GO BAD!

NAMOR'S CABAL
Namor secretly works with Iron Man, Mister Fantastic, Black Panther, Beast and Black Bolt to prevent a clash of worlds destroying Earth. When the others reject his drastic solutions, Namor betrays them and joins a Cabal of ruthless villains!

NEPTUNE'S TRIDENT
The ruler of Atlantis often uses the trident as a standard, and it can also **manipulate water** and fire powerful **mystical beams.**

TOP 3
Most Powerful Beings

1 **FRANKLIN RICHARDS** – the son of Susan and Reed Richards can manipulate reality, molecules, time and even see the future!

2 **PROTEUS** – warps reality, and can take over a human body as his host.

3 **APOCALYPSE** – can bring about (you guessed it!) the apocalypse!

TELL ME MORE!

The Multiverse must remain balanced or all will be destroyed! Master Order and Lord Chaos push and pull their servant, the In-Betweener, who must work to balance their desires. If all else fails, the Living Tribunal can intervene to keep the peace.

ALWAYS WATCHING...

THE WATCHERS are an ALL-SEEING alien race who vow to observe the universe, but NEVER INTERVENE. UATU THE WATCHER gives occasional warnings to humanity, but still keeps COSMIC SECRETS. This leads to his MURDER and the countless mysteries hidden within his eyes being REVEALED!

BETWEEN...

The most powerful character in the Multiverse is the One-Above-All. Not only does he possess more power than any known entity, he is believed to represent the writers and artists of Marvel Comics!

...THE PANELS

NOoooo!! The omnipotent **BEYONDER** uses Earth's heroes and villains as playthings! He creates **"SECRET WARS"** on his **BATTLEWORLD** (a planet of his own creation) and forces Super Heroes and Villains to fight each other!

▲ **ETERNITY** – embodies time

TOP 4 COSMIC ENTITIES

They exist outside of everything and possess vast powers over space, time and existence.

INFINITY – embodies the entirety of space

DEATH – can give and take life as she pleases

OBLIVION – embodies all that is nothingness

POWER PLAYERS

S.H.I.E.L.D. DECLASSIFIED

CYTTORAK, LORD OF OBLIVION
Cyttorak may be the strongest magical being in the Multiverse. Not only is his name so powerful that it is spoken as part of spells, but one of his gems is the source of the Juggernaut's powers. Cyttorak even has the strength to imprison Galactus, Devourer of Worlds.

TOP 3 MIGHTY MYTHICAL MASTERS

YAO, THE ANCIENT ONE – the mystical master and teacher of Doctor Strange

LEI-KUNG THE THUNDERER – immortal martial arts mentor of Iron Fist

CHTHON – Dark Elder God; created vampires and responsible for the powers of sorceress Morgan le Fay.

Power Up!

COSMIC UPGRADE
Cosmic power can have a **DARK SIDE!** **JEAN GREY** is a powerful telepath, but after absorbing the **PHOENIX FORCE**, she becomes **PHOENIX** – wielding the power to obliterate or create **ENTIRE PLANETS!**

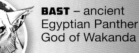
TOP 5 POWERFUL GODS

BAST – ancient Egyptian Panther God of Wakanda

ZEUS – Godhead of Olympus

GAEA – Elder God and Mother Earth

AMATSU-MIKABOSHI – Shinto God of Chaos

ODIN – All-Father of Asgard

TELL ME MORE!

The Vishanti (Hoggoth the Hoary, Oshtur and Agamotto) are an ancient, magical trinity who have protected the Earthly dimensions since the dawn of time! They pen the mystical Book of the Vishanti that helps Doctor Strange become Sorcerer Supreme.

REALLY?!

The **Supreme Intelligence** may be a supercomputer, but it's one of the most **powerful beings** in the Multiverse! It is created by the Kree, an advanced alien race, but develops **a mind of its own**. Its ruthless logic then results in the **destruction** of the Kree homeworld!

AAARRGHH!!
GRANDMASTER is a virtually immortal cosmic being. He travels the universe **MASTERING GAMES** of all kinds. He even challenges **DEATH** to a game, **AND WINS!**

These **all-powerful** masters of the **cosmic** and **mystical** realms balance the forces of good and evil, chaos and order, time and space. They could end the **entire Multiverse** – or **create a new one!**

Golden Avenger

Endo-Sym Armour

Silver Centurion

The Red/Gold Armour

WOW!

52

...and counting! The number of different Iron Man suits.

War Machine's Armour

Classic Gray Armour

Iron Destroyer Armour

Hulkbuster Armour

Stealth Armour MK II

Space Armour MK III

Iconic Armour

Hydro Suit

Model 42 Armour

HEAVY METAL

Tony Stark is the **billionaire owner** of tech company Stark Industries, a **playboy** and **world-class genius!** His many **suits of armour** control a life-threatening injury and grant him **amazing powers** to fight for justice as **Iron Man!**

BETWEEN...

Marvel's Stan Lee wanted to create a character – a rich arms manufacturer – readers would dislike, and make him sympathetic. Iron Man duly debuted in *Tales of Suspense* #39 (March 1963)!

...THE PANELS

FAST FACTS

REAL NAME: Anthony Edward Stark

STRENGTHS: Genius-level intellect, leadership, engineering skills, combat skills

WEAKNESSES: often needs tech to stay alive; alcohol problems; big ego

POWER SOURCE: Iron Man suits enhance durability and strength, fire repulsor blasts, and grant supersonic flight

FOES: Too many to mention!

ALLIES: War Machine/ Iron Patriot (Jim Rhodes), Avengers, Mr Fantastic

TELL ME MORE!

Critically wounded and held hostage by a warlord, Tony Stark and fellow prisoner Ho Yinsen construct a magnetic plate that prevents shrapnel in Tony's chest from reaching his heart. The magnet also powers a suit of armour...

BEST KNOWN FOR

CONTROL FREAKERY AND PARTYING

IDENTITY CRISIS!

Jim "Rhodey" Rhodes dons the Iron Man armour to protect Tony's secret identity, before stepping into his own identity as the heavily armed War Machine.

WOW!

12,348

The speed that Iron Man's Space Armor MK III can reach, in kph (7,673mph).

Power Up!

GOING TO EXTREMES

Tony enhances his system with **EXTREMIS NANOTECH**, enabling him to store his armour's under layer **IN HIS BONES**. He gains strength, agility and can grow **NEW ORGANS**!

S.H.I.E.L.D. DECLASSIFIED

DIRECTOR STARK

Following the superhuman civil war, Tony Stark is appointed director of S.H.I.E.L.D. When he fails to anticipate and to prevent the alien Skrulls' invasion of Earth, his reputation is severely damaged, and the villainous Norman Osborn takes his place.

UNLUCKY IN LOVE

Playboy Tony is famous for his stormy love affairs. He has a knack for getting involved with beautiful women who have shady agendas, psychological issues, can't cope with him being Iron Man or get killed!

WHEN GOOD GUYS GO BAD!

Caught in the Red Skull's "inversion wave", the bad aspects of Tony's character come to the fore. Choosing profit over heroism, Tony develops an Extremis 3.0 app and charges civilians outrageous sums to use its enhancing nanotech.

RESCUE MISSION

An attack by Ezekiel Stane leaves Tony's some time girlfriend Pepper Potts with shrapnel in her chest. Tony saves her life by equipping her with a special Iron Man suit, allowing her to become the hero Rescue!

NOOOOO!!

TONY'S ARMOUR develops a mind of its own and begins using **LETHAL FORCE**. Confronting his "living armour," Tony has a heart attack and the armour sacrifices its sentience to **SAVE HIM**!

TOP 5

Iron Man Suits

1 **HULKBUSTER** – lets Tony go toe-to-green-toe with an out-of-control Hulk.

2 **IRON DESTROYER** – Uru-powered upgrade – handy when Thor's evil uncle attacks Earth.

3 **STEALTH ARMOUR MK II** – equipped with "active camouflage" – you can't fight what you can't see!

4 **SPACE ARMOUR MK III** – back-mounted rocket thrusters and an onboard A.I. called P.E.P.P.E.R. enable Tony to be a true Guardian of the Galaxy.

5 **HYDRO SUIT** – this pressure-resistant model allows Stark to get wet and wild in the depths of the ocean.

KEY ARMOURED FOES

CRIMSON DYNAMO
Everything is bigger in Russia, as proven by this walking Soviet tank. Bigger, but not necessarily better!

WHIPLASH
This highly talented techie takes a piece of Tony Stark's armour and adds his own deadly electrified whips.

SPYMASTER
The face behind the mask may change, but every single Spymaster spells major trouble for Tony.

BLIZZARD
Is it suddenly freezing cold, or is it just Blizzard's ability to generate sub-zero temperatures?

WHIRLWIND
Imagine a spinning top covered with razor blades and you've got this tornado-generating super-thug.

IRON MONGER
Munitions dealer Obadiah Stane tries to gain control of Stark Industries by attacking in his Iron Monger armour.

TELL ME MORE!

Hank Pym discovers Pym Particles. These allow him to shrink to ant-size (or even smaller), or grow to enormous heights! The serum can be taken as a pill or breathed in as a gas.

30.5

Hank Pym's max size as Goliath/ Giant-Man in metres (100ft).

S.H.I.E.L.D. DECLASSIFIED

AVENGERS A.I.
The robot Ultron isn't Hank Pym's only disastrous invention. He also develops an anti-Ultron virus that evolves into a sentient A.I., calling itself Dimitrios. This becomes such a threat that Hank forms an Avengers A.I. team (Hank, Doombot, Alexis, Vision, Victor Mancha and Monica Chang) specially to combat it.

HANK PYM – FUGITIVE

Hank's enemy **Egghead** frames him for stealing **nuclear secrets.** Egghead and the Masters of Evil then **break him out** during the trial, making things look **even worse** for Hank!

AAARRGHH!!
Hank's **BIGGEST MISTAKE** is creating the robot Ultron. Ultron **COMES ALIVE,** wants to kill the entire human race, and has a **CRUSH** on Hank's wife, Wasp!

"I'm not Ant-Man anymore."

"I'm not Giant-Man..."

WHAT?!

When Hank dumps his **shy Giant-Man persona** and becomes **brash vigilante Yellowjacket,** he doesn't tell his Avengers team or his **girlfriend Janet.** Yellowjacket kisses her and, to **everyone's amazement,** she agrees to **marry him!**

Q: How Does Hank Pym Control Ants?

A: Hank develops a **cybernetic helmet** to control ants. The helmet transmits **psionic and electronic waves** and has a broadcast range of **1.6km (1 mile).** Hank first calls on ants for help when KGB agents try to **kill** him and **destroy** his research.

BACK FROM THE DEAD!

Hank and Ultron eventually **merge!** Hank realises what he has become and seemingly **dies.** Months later, he's back, wearing Ultron as **armour!**

PYM'S PARTICLES

Hank Pym is a brilliant **scientist**, **robotics expert** and a founding member of **the Avengers.** But whether shrinking as **Ant-Man** or hitting the heights **as Goliath,** he's never felt **at ease** being a Super Hero!

BAD DAY

Hank consumes so many Pym Particles that he can change size at will and even alter the size of any objects he touches! However, this proves bad for his health.

"...or Goliath..."

"...or Yellow-jacket!"

BEST KNOWN FOR

CHANGING HIS SIZE AND HIS HERO ID

"I'M HENRY PYM!"

FAST FACTS

REAL NAME:
Dr Henry "Hank" Pym

ALIASES: Ant-Man, Goliath, Giant-Man, Yellowjacket, Wasp, Ultron

STRENGTHS: Brilliant scientist and inventor

WEAKNESSES: Insecure, jealous of other heroes, guilt complex, work puts strain on his health

ALLIES: Avengers, West Coast Avengers, Mighty Avengers, Tigra, Wasp

FOES: Egghead, Kang, Morgan Le Fay, Ultron

IDENTITY CRISIS!

Hank Pym is replaced by a Skrull imposter during the Secret Wars. The real Hank returns, only to see his wife Janet die, owing to the evil deeds of the Skrull agent. Hank takes on her Wasp Super Hero identity in her honour.

FAST FACTS

REAL NAME:
Janet Van Dyne

STRENGTHS: Changing size, superhuman speed, flight, bio-electric blasts

WEAKNESSES: Shrinking too small could trap her in the Microverse!

FOES: Yellowjacket (Criti Noll), Egghead

FAMOUS RELATIVE: Dr Hank Pym (ex-husband)

NUMBER CRUNCH!

1.6m (5ft 4in)
Janet Van Dyne's height

1.3m or less (4ft 2in or less)
Height when wings begin to sprout

1.3cm (0.5 in)
Janet's miniature height as Wasp

50kg (110lbs)
Wasp's weight

2–4 wings
Wasp's varying number of wings

63kph (38mph)
Wasp's approximate flight speed

REALLY?!

Hank Pym implants cells in Janet's head that allow her to grow **temporary antennae** and communicate with insects!

HANDLE WITH CARE!

Yellowjacket (Hank Pym) gives Janet the **Power Prism** and it takes control of her mind! The gem is really a **sentient being** with the power to manipulate energy.

BAD DAY

Janet **divorces** Hank Pym when the effects of regularly **shrinking and growing** change his personality, making him **jealous and paranoid.**

"HI! I'm the Wasp! And you've just been **STUNG!**"

30
The weight Wasp can lift in tons at her max size.

BACK FROM THE DEAD!

The world believes Wasp has been **killed,** but after her emergency signal comes from the **Microverse,** the Avengers shrink down and **rescue her!**

AAARRGHH!! During the **SKRULL INVASION,** Wasp gets trapped in the **MICROVERSE!** However, Hank and the Avengers presume she is **KILLED IN BATTLE** so don't think to look for her!

BEFORE...

In order to heal Janet from serious injuries, Hank Pym places her inside a cocoon to recuperate. When she emerges, Janet is more wasp than human, with massive wings, long antennae and spindly fingers! Hank assures the concerned Avengers that Janet is in "perfect physical health!"

AFTER...

TELL ME MORE!

Thanks to Pym Particles, Wasp can grow and shrink at will, just like Ant-Man. Wasp's insect-like wings sprout when she shrinks below normal size, and they are absorbed by her body as she grows. She can also emit bio-electric blasts ("wasp stings") from her hands to stun opponents.

SUPER STING!

Janet Van Dyne joins forces with Hank Pym to avenge the death of her father, becoming the amazing **Wasp!** She is also a **founding member** of the **Avengers**, inspiring her teammates with courage and determination. She's tiny, but with a serious sting!

Q: How does Janet become the Wasp?

A: Janet's father, Vernon, uses a **gamma radiation beam** to search for alien life. A **Kosmosian criminal** follows the beam to Earth and murders Vernon. Janet wants to **avenge** her father, so Hank Pym transforms her into **the Wasp!**

Power Up!

TALL TALE
Janet spends most of her transformations as the **TINY WASP**, but after a **ROMANCE WITH HAWKEYE**, she decides it's time for a **BIG CHANGE!** She tries out the high life **AS A GIANT!**

Q: How does Scott become Ant-Man?

A: He steals the **old suit** of the original Ant-Man, inventor **Hank Pym.** Scott also steals Hank's Pym Particle formula to shrink to **ant size.**

Q: Why does Scott become Ant-Man?

A: Scott's young daughter **Cassie** needs a **heart op** but the surgeon has been kidnapped. **Desperate measures** are called for!

BEST KNOWN FOR

GETTING TO PLACES OTHER HEROES CAN'T REACH

THINK SMALL!

Super Heroes can come in **small sizes!** It's all very well being able to **punch out** a villain, don an **iron battle suit** or wield a **magic hammer...** but sometimes, **big problems** call for a tiny hero – **Ant-Man!**

NOOOOOO!!

Scott's daughter, Cassie, follows her father into the hero business as the size-changing **STATURE**, but is killed by a super-powered **DOCTOR DOOM**!

WOW

1.6

Distance in km that Ant-Man can talk to insects (1,760 yards). Of course, he needs to be wearing his cybernetic helmet!

YESSS!!

Ant-Man **SAVES** his daughter Cassie's life during her heart transplant by **SHRINKING** to microscopic size and attacking her **WHITE BLOOD CELLS**!

Ride 'em Ant-Man!
If Scott wants to get **somewhere super-fast,** he just shrinks himself to bug size and jumps aboard **a friendly flying ant!**

"Truth is, I've always been kind of a lousy *SUPER HERO.*"

FAST FACTS

REAL NAME:
Scott Edward Harris Lang

STRENGTHS: Gaseous Pym Particles in belt allow him to shrink to any size; helmet enables control of insects; wrist gauntlets fire bio-electric blasts; electronics expert; a good dad

WEAKNESSES: Low self-esteem, for a hero; only possesses the strength of a normal man; can be squashed

FRIENDS: Avengers, Fantastic Four

FOES: Taskmaster, Master of Evil

NEW START

Scott puts his **criminal past** to good use when he starts a private security firm – **Ant-Man Security Solutions**. He runs the company himself, with help from **a team of ants** and a former foe – bear-exo-skeleton-wearing **Grizzly!**

Clint's Sarcastic Sayings

1. "Cap, did you *TAKE LESSONS* on how to be a *CORNBALL*, or does it just *COME NATURAL?*"

2. "I like playing *DUMB*. It makes me *FEEL SMART. SOMETIMES.*"

3. "Figured you hadn't had one of these in a long time... *A PARTY* I mean, not birthdays. You gotta be at *LEAST EIGHTY* or something."

4. "*FLATMAN??* I don't believe it! You got a partner called '*RIBBON*'?"

5. "*FIRST SIGN* of madness. *TALKIN'* to yourself. *FISHING'S* the SECOND.*"

"Well, here's another fine mess you've gotten us into *Hawkeye!*"

TEAM PLAYER
Clint is **not comfortable** taking orders, leading to **frequent spats** with Captain America. Despite the conflicts, Cap recognises Hawkeye's **leadership potential** and appoints him to **head up** a team of **Secret Avengers** including Captain Britain, Venom, Valkyrie and the original Human Torch.

Clint has dated **many** of his heroic colleagues, including the Wasp, Scarlet Witch, Spider-Woman and Black Widow – who leads him into a shady world of spying before both reform and become Avengers!

CUPID'S ARROW

IDENTITY CRISIS?

Clint gets fed up with not having superpowers, so he doses himself with Pym Particles and grows to giant proportions, becoming the Super Hero Goliath! It doesn't last, though – Clint realises you don't need powers to be a hero!

HOT SHOT!

Hawkeye is a **mainstay** of the **Avengers**, but he has a chip on his shoulder **bigger than the Hulk** – he's got **no superpowers!** Earth's Mightiest Heroes wouldn't be the same, though, without the purple-clad sharpshooter's wit and **ace archery skills!**

FAMOUS LAST WORDS

"COME ON AVENGERS! Let's end this OUR way!!"

–JUST BEFORE HAWKEYE FLIES INTO A KREE WARSHIP'S ENGINE TO SAVE THE TEAM.

DOG'S DINNER
When Clint moves to Brooklyn, he **rescues a dog** named **Arrow** from a pack of criminals. Clint renames him **Lucky**, but the pooch's penchant for pizza earns him the nickname **Pizza Dog!**

FAMILY CONNECTIONS
Clint's brother Barney is content being a **small-time hustler** until Baron Zemo manipulates him into becoming the villain **Trickshot**. He joins the Dark Avengers, but villainy doesn't work out so well: he shows up on Clint's doorstep seeking forgiveness – **and a few coins!**

FAST FACTS

REAL NAME:
Clinton Francis "Clint" Barton

STRENGTHS:
Master archer, expert marksman, martial artist

WEAPONS: His custom-made bow and a trick arrow for every situation

ALLIES: Black Widow, Iron Man, Captain America, Mockingbird

CLAIM TO FAME:
His arrows never miss!

"When you talk to the **COPS** about this, tell 'em Hawkeye was the **GOOD GUY** willya? I don't need any more **BAD PRESS**."

TELL ME MORE!

Hawkeye may have the best eyes in the business, but after he uses a sonic arrow to defeat the villainous Crossfire, he goes deaf! It doesn't last forever though – his hearing is restored when Franklin Richards alters reality.

WOW!

122

The number of arrow types Hawkeye uses (there could be even more – it's tough for him to keep count!).

TOP 7
Best Arrows

1 **EXPLOSIVE ARROW** – *KA-BLAM!*

2 **ROCKET ARROW** – blasts away the bad guys!

3 **BOXING GLOVE ARROW** – a knockout!

4 **PYM PARTICLES ARROW** – shrinks your target right off the battlefield.

5 **HACKING ARROW** – for when you can't remember your computer password.

6 **GLUE ARROW** – puts bad guys in a sticky situation!

7 **BOOMERANG ARROW** – really cuts down on restocking costs.

Power Up!

HAWKEYE'S "WINGS"
Since Hawkeye **CAN'T FLY**, he asks an engineer to build him an **ANTIGRAVITY SKY-CYCLE**! He then uses it to **FLY** into battle – **IN STYLE**!

BACK FROM THE DEAD!

Clint **sacrifices** himself to stop the Kree invasion, but is brought **back to life** when Scarlet Witch **alters reality**.

290

Thor's weight in kg (640lbs).
He's only 2m (6ft 6in),
but Asgardian muscle and
bone is incredibly dense.

GOD OF THUNDER!

FAST FACTS

REAL NAME: Thor Odinson

STRENGTHS: Immensely strong, warrior skills, heroically handsome

WEAKNESSES: Needs his hammer, Mjolnir, to fly, manipulate weather, fire energy blasts

FOES: Loki, Malekith, Enchantress

ALLIES: Captain America, Warriors Three (Fandral the Dashing, Hogun the Grim, Volstagg the Valiant)

BACK FROM THE DEAD!

Tony Stark believes Thor is dead, so he creates a **clone version** from one of Thor's hairs! This violent version is called **Ragnarok**.

Oh, Brother!

Thor doesn't get along with his adopted brother, **Loki, God of Mischief**. Only brotherly love has stopped them killing each other – **so far!**

Name Game

Spider-Man's nickname for Thor is **Goldilocks!**

"The *legend* has come true!"

By the *will of the GODS, I am alive!*

I am invincible! I am – *THOR!!!"*

1,000,000

The weight of an arch Thor once destroyed, in tons.

KAPOW!

In battle, Thor can increase his strength **tenfold** by entering into a state known as **Warrior's Madness!**

Asgardians aren't immortal. Thor has eaten a Golden Apple of Idunn, which grants him long-lasting life!

REALLY?!

Thor's chariot is drawn by two flying goats called **Toothgnasher** and **Toothgrinder.**

AFTER...

BEFORE...

TOP 3

Thor's Human Identities

1 **DONALD BLAKE** – a doctor
2 **SIGURD JARLSON** – a construction worker
3 **JAKE OLSON** – a deceased thief and former paramedic

HANDLE WITH CARE!

Thor owes much of his power to his magical hammer, **Mjolnir**. You have to be **"worthy"** to wield Mjolnir, and sometimes Thor **just isn't worthy enough!**

ALTERNATE UNIVERSE

The evil scientists of **A.I.M.** recruit a villainous version of Thor named **Thorr** from another dimension. Thorr's Mjolnir can only be lifted by someone who's **unworthy!**

Q: Who's tougher – Thor or the Hulk?

A: When Thor faces off in **hand-to-hand** combat against the **Incredible Hulk**, the Green Giant gets covered in **tons of rock**. It's not clear who the winner is, so let's call it a **draw!**

ASGARD AVENGER

Thor isn't just **the Norse God of Thunder**—he is also the protector of the realms of his home world, **Asgard**. With his hammer, **Mjolnir**, Thor rains thunder and lightning down on his enemies. No wonder he's one of the **most powerful** Super Heroes around!

Thor, Goddess of Thunder

When Mjolnir judges Thor unworthy, the mystical hammer chooses Jane Foster – Thor's **ex-girlfriend** – to wield its power. Thor passes his mantle on to her, making Jane the all-new Mighty Thor!

BETWEEN...

Looking for a new character, Marvel's Stan Lee turned to his favourite Norse myths. In August 1962, Thor the Thunder God was reborn as a comic book Super Hero!

...THE PANELS

HIGH FLYER

Hard work, fierce independence and phenomenal willpower help Carol Danvers become Captain Marvel – one of Earth's greatest heroes. Whether she's soaring through space or facing foes, Captain Marvel's first priority is to protect the planet.

TEAM PLAYER

When Captain Marvel isn't joining up with **Guardians of the Galaxy**, she splits her time between female Avengers team **A-Force** and powerhouse squad the **Ultimates!**

REALLY?!

Captain Marvel's pet cat, **Chewie**, is actually a **Flerken** – an **extremely dangerous, egg-laying alien** who just happens to resemble Earth felines. Luckily, Chewie is just as **cuddly** as a typical kitty.

TELL ME MORE!

Carol Danvers is caught in the explosion of an alien device known as the "Psyche-Magnetron". Her genetic structure mingles with that of the heroic Kree alien, Mar-Vell, granting her superhuman abilities!

UPGRADED!

Thanks to genetic tampering by aliens, Carol gains a connection to a white hole – and the energies of a star! She becomes the cosmic hero Binary.

YESSS!!

Carol is a former **AIR FORCE CAPTAIN**. Her **MILITARY EXPERTISE** makes her the ideal candidate to lead a new **SPACE DEFENCE** programme against alien threats with team **ALPHA FLIGHT**.

"Even with my back against the wall— I DON'T GIVE UP!"

REAL NAME: Carol Danvers

ALIASES: Ms Marvel, Binary, Warbird

FOES: Deathbird, Yon-Rogg, Moonstone

ALLIES: Mar-Vell, Ms Marvel (Kamala Khan), Rogue, Spider-Woman

POWERS: Flight, superhuman strength, durability, agility, fires energy blasts from hands

ARCHENEMIES
Captain Marvel frequently fights Shi'ar villainess, **Deathbird.** This menacing foe doesn't just boast razor-sharp **telescopic javelins** – she also knows and exploits Carol's **greatest weakness:** putting others' welfare **before her own safety.**

WOW!
117
The number of eggs Chewie lays on Captain Marvel's spaceship. They hatch into kittens!

NEXT GENERATION
When teenager **Kamala Khan's** Inhuman **shape-shifting** abilities kick in, she's **inspired** by her hero Carol Danvers to become the **new Ms Marvel** and **fight crime** in Jersey City!

BETWEEN...
Writer Kelly Sue DeConnick's long stint on *Captain Marvel* was so popular that fans began calling themselves the "Carol Corps"!

...THE PANELS

NOooooo!!
In a long-awaited rematch, Captain Marvel defeats her Kree nemesis, **YON-ROGG.** But victory comes at a price – she **LOSES** most of her **MEMORIES!**

ALTERNATE UNIVERSE
In the Marvel **Mangaverse**, a nearly invulnerable Carol Danvers dons the costume, shield and moniker of **Captain America!**

Ms Marvel

A young girl who idolises Carol gives her the nickname "Princess Sparklefists". It's unlikely she will ditch "Captain Marvel" for that title any time soon...

BEFORE...
When Carol steps into the role of Captain Marvel, she **ditches** her lightning-bolt leotard for a **sleek new suit** that better represents her **military background** and **years of heroic experience.**

Ms Marvel/ Warbird

Binary

Captain Marvel

AFTER...

"My name is... Madame Natasha... but you... can call me *THE BLACK WIDOW!*"

NUMBER CRUNCH!

1928
Black Widow's approximate birth year (she doesn't age)

1.70m (5ft 7in)
Height

59kg (131lbs)
Weight

6.1+m (20+ft)
Range of "Widow's bite"

1.8kg (4lbs)
of Dynamite – equivalent in plastic explosives carried by Black Widow

WOW!

30,000
Max charge in volts of Natasha's "Widow's Bite".

WHEN BAD GUYS Go GOOD!

FRENEMIES

Black Widow is sent by the Russian KGB to spy on Stark Industries. She fakes a romance with Tony Stark, but he soon gets wise. Natasha switches sides and becomes one of Iron Man's most trusted allies!

BLACK WIDOWERS: NATASHA'S EXES

1 Natasha marries **ALEXI SHOSTAKOV**, but the K.G.B. fakes his death and trains him as the Red Guardian super-soldier!

2 Natasha and **MATT MURDOCK** (Daredevil) move in together. She leaves though, and founds Super Hero team The Champions of Los Angeles.

3 At first, Natasha is a bad influence on **HAWKEYE**. They have a brief, but fiery romance. He even proposes!

REALLY?!

The man who raised Natasha, **Ivan Petrovich**, becomes an insane **cyborg**, and she is forced to destroy him!

"If the world learns I am the *BLACK WIDOW*, it would mean the *END* of my private life!

I should have *CONSIDERED* that when I designed my *MASKLESS NEW COSTUME!*"

S.H.I.E.L.D. DECLASSIFIED

THE BLACK WIDOWS
The Red Room is a programme run by the KGB that trains female spies known as "Black Widows". They are implanted with false memories and given a version of the Super-Soldier serum to enhance their physical abilities and slow aging.

FAST FACTS

REAL NAME: Natalia Alianovna Romanova (a.k.a. Natasha Romanoff)

STRENGTHS: Master martial artist and acrobat; a version of the Super-Soldier serum keeps her in peak physical condition

WEAKNESSES: Her dark and uncertain past

FOES: Hydra, Gynacon Corporation, Baron Von Strucker, Yelena Belova

TOP 4

Influences On Black Widow

1 **HAWKEYE** – convinces Natasha to defect to S.H.I.E.L.D.

2 **CAPTAIN AMERICA** – saves Natasha's life when she is a girl. Later recruits her to the Avengers.

3 **IRON MAN** – Natasha sides with Stark during the superhuman civil war.

4 **BUCKY BARNES** – trains Natasha as a Black Widow.

Q: Who is Yelena Belova?

A: Belova is a recent graduate of the KGB's **Red Room**, with higher grades than Natasha. She works for terrorist group **Hydra**, who transform her into a powerful **Super-Adaptoid android** – then trigger her to **self-destruct!**

KAPOW!

Black Widow uses automatic weapons and knives, but she is famous for her **Widow's Bite** (electric bolts to disable her enemies) and the **Widow's Line** (a cable for swinging and climbing).

BACK FROM THE DEAD!

While on a mission, Natasha is poisoned and killed by the **Hand** ninjas! Stone – an ally of Daredevil's – magically brings her **back to life.**

AARRGHH!!

Natasha thinks she's had a **GREAT CAREER** as a ballerina, but it's a **FALSE MEMORY** planted by **THE K.G.B.!**

SUPER SPY

The Black Widow is trained as a **lethal sleeper agent** by the K.G.B. and sent to the U.S.A. But her Russian spy career is short-lived – she **turns away from skulduggery** and uses her amazing espionage skills as **a heroic Avenger!**

The Black Panther is a hereditary title, but it must be earned through trials. When T'Challa is deemed unworthy by the Panther God, his younger sister, Shuri, steps up to lead the country as the new Black Panther.

Black Panther gains many powers from the juice of the **Heart-Shaped Herb.** It is said that the herb will **kill** anyone not **worthy enough!**

"It is not for nothing that I am called the *BLACK PANTHER!*"

AAAARRGHH!!

ULYSSES KLAW wants Wakanda's **VIBRANIUM** and slays T'Chaka, T'Challa's father. T'Challa shatters Klaw's right hand and **EJECTS** the outsider from the country.

CLAW OF THE JUNGLE

Ruler. Diplomat. Warrior. Avenger. Black Panther is all of these – protecting the great African nation of **Wakanda** from the outside world, and using his intellect and power to **fight injustice** across the globe.

Power Up!

HEART AND SOUL
T'Challa shares a connection to the mysterious **PANTHER GOD.** This grants him enhanced senses and an **INSTINCTIVE CONNECTION** to his homeland, **WAKANDA.**

When Black Panther first meets **the Fantastic Four,** he shows off his skills by **defeating** each one of them!

REVENGE!
During a **universe-destroying** Incursion, T'Challa **takes revenge on Namor** for the destruction of Wakanda – by **abandoning the** aquatic hero on a dying planet!

BETWEEN...
Black Panther debuted in *Fantastic Four #52* (July 1966), making him one of comics' first black Super Heroes. Created by Stan Lee and Jack Kirby, the character gained his own title in 1973.

...THE PANELS

After a **long romance,** T'Challa and Storm **finally wed** on the **eve of the civil war,** but break up when the Phoenix Force **possesses** five X-Men, resulting in **Wakanda's destruction!**

LOVED – AND LOST...

ALTERNATE UNIVERSE

In the ravaged world of **Earth X,** T'Challa has been mutated by **Terrigen Mists** into a **true** humanoid black panther!

TOP 5

Black Panther Foes

1 **ULYSSES KLAW** – murders Black Panther's father and tries to steal Wakanda's vibranium ore.

2 **NAMOR** – destroys Wakanda with a huge tidal wave.

3 **MAN-APE** – eats the sacred White Gorilla and gains its powers.

4 **KILLMONGER** – wants to overthrow T'Challa and rule Wakanda.

5 **WHITE WOLF** – adopted by T'Challa's father; one-time leader of Wakanda's brutal secret police.

S.H.I.E.L.D. DECLASSIFIED

VIBRANIUM OF WAKANDA
T'Challa rules Wakanda, an isolated and advanced African nation. Wakanda is known for its technological innovation and its vast source of the rare and almost indestructible Vibranium ore. The metal is used to line Black Panther's suit and allows his claws to cut almost anything.

FAST FACTS

REAL NAME: T'Challa

HOME COUNTRY: Wakanda

STRENGTHS: Genius-level intellect, enhanced senses, Olympic-level strength and reflexes, skilled tracker, Vibranium suit

WEAKNESSES: Bright lights and loud noises can overpower his senses

RELATIVES: Storm (ex-wife), Shuri (younger sister and successor), T'Chaka (predecessor and father)

ELECTRIC ATTRACTION
Matt Murdock and Elektra Natchios are college sweethearts – until her father is murdered. Elektra becomes an assassin for hire! She reenters Matt's life when secret ninja organisation the Hand tries to kill him.

IDENTITY CRISIS?

"Sometimes I think I was born to be Daredevil – and Matt Murdock is the identity that's not for real!"

"The name's *DAREDEVIL...* remember it!"

NIGHTTIME NINJA

By day, **blind Matt Murdock** works as an **attorney**. By night, he's **Daredevil**, protecting the **innocent** from crime and Super Villains! To law-abiding folks he's a **guardian angel**, but to the criminals of the underworld he's a **terror**!

WOW!

15

The maximum distance in metres (50ft) Daredevil can track a person by smell through a crowd.

TELL ME MORE!

SUPER SENSITIVE
A childhood accident with radioactive chemicals leaves Matt blind but boosts his other senses to amazing levels. He can hear changes in a person's heartbeat that reveal they are lying! He also develops a "Radar Sense" that perceives the 3-D space around him and detects motion.

REAL NAME: Matthew (Matt) Michael Murdock

STRENGTHS: Incredible martial arts, superhuman senses, athletic skills

WEAKNESS: Legally blind

JOB: Trial lawyer

HOME TURF: Hell's Kitchen (New York City)

ALLIES: Spider-Man, Black Widow, Iron Fist, Foggy Nelson, Karen Page

FOES: Kingpin, Bullseye, Stilt-Man, Electro, Impossible Man

REALLY?!

Daredevil's sense of touch is so **fine-tuned** he can **read newsprint** just by **feeling it!**

BETWEEN...

When creating Daredevil, Stan Lee wanted a fresh new Super Hero formula. He focused on a hero with a great weakness, who had developed amazing powers to compensate.

...THE PANELS

BEST KNOWN FOR
HUNTING DOWN UNDERWORLD BOSS KINGPIN

NUMBER CRUNCH!

20mg
The amount of a substance needed in food for Daredevil to detect it.

12 years old
The age Matt Murdock loses his sight.

6m (20ft)
The maximum distance Daredevil can hear a heartbeat.

3 city blocks
The maximum distance Daredevil can smell gunpowder.

1 decibel
The lowest sounds Daredevil can hear (20 for average people).

KAPOW!

Matt's father is a **boxer** who wants his young son to stick to his studies. However, Matt disobeys and secretly becomes a **martial artist,** trained in **ninjitsu, kung fu** and **karate** by mysterious mentor Stick.

TOP 3

Daredevil Fill-Ins

1 IRON FIST – poses as Daredevil while Matt is in prison, and during the Civil War.

2 PETER PARKER – dresses as Daredevil to protect Matt's identity in court, until another Daredevil imposter, actor Terrence Hillman, also shows up!

3 FOGGY NELSON – pretends to be Daredevil to romance Matt's on-off girlfriend Karen Page!

Q: Is Daredevil a lone wolf crime fighter?

A: No – he sometimes teams up with **Spider-Man,** who **patrols** some of the same areas. He turns down several invitations to join **the Avengers,** but finally comes aboard after urging from **Luke Cage.**

DAREDEVIL'S GUIDE TO SNAZZY COSTUMES

Stand Out!
A yellow suit with a single "D" insignia (later double) gives a distinctive look.

Keep It Simple!
Comfort is key for Super Heroes! This crimson suit is a practical choice.

Arm Yourself!
Guard against injury with this biomimetic suit with in-built white armour.

Switch It Up!
This black costume with red utility belt and gloves is sure to freak out foes.

HANDLE WITH CARE!

Matt's **cane** contains a **grappling hook** and **cable** for climbing rooftops. It also converts into a **fighting club,** and he can **throw** it with incredible accuracy.

TELL ME MORE!

With their world on the brink of destruction, the Korbinites transform their most powerful warrior, Beta Ray Bill, into a cybernetic super-being. He travels the galaxy for aid and finds it in Asgard, where Odin gives him the Uru hammer Stormbreaker and similar powers to his son, Thor.

183

...and counting! The number of known alien races in the Marvel Universe.

Q: What happens when a planet comes to life?

A: You get **Ego the Living Planet!** Using powerful humanoids created from his **own body,** Ego attacks other worlds and **absorbs them** into himself!

Power Up!

NOVA PRIME
Rhomann Dey, the last of the **NOVA CORPS,** gives Earth's Richard Rider the power of **NOVA PRIME.** Richard goes from working in a **BURGER BAR** to fighting evil and **PROTECTING THE GALAXY** as the super-strong and invulnerable **NOVA!**

YECCH!

Knowhere is treated like a planet, but it's actually the enormous rotting head of an ancient Celestial! The inhabitants of Knowhere mine the head for its rare and precious resources – such as bone and brain!

S.H.I.E.L.D. DECLASSIFIED

ADAM WARLOCK
Adam Warlock is created by the Beehive, a group of evil scientists, to be a physically perfect human. He rebels against his creators and uses the powerful Soul Gem, given to him by the High Evolutionary, to protect the universe from cosmic threats.

HANDLE WITH CARE!

If you're looking for the **most powerful** items in the universe, go see **the Collector,** Taneleer Tivan. An **Elder of the Universe,** he's one of the oldest known beings in the cosmos and spends his life collecting **items of boundless power.**

BLAST OFF!

There's a universe of **cosmic wonders** out there! Mighty alien heroes, **godly beings** with supreme powers, creatures the **size of planets** – there's a lot more to space than just **rockets and astronauts!**

GUARDIAN OF THE UNIVERSE

The **Uni-Power** is a manifestation of the universe itself! When **reality is in peril** it bonds with a host to become **Captain Universe** – a hero tasked with protecting **everything in existence!**

ALTERNATE UNIVERSE

The **Uni-Power** doesn't discriminate about its partners. On Earth-91110, it bonds with a **dog** named Casey to become **Captain Uni-Mutt!**

TELL ME MORE!

Eon is a cosmic entity hailing from his own dimension, the Eonverse. He creates the powerful Quantum Bands and appoints the Protectors of the Universe to wield them.

REAL NAME:
Dr Robert Bruce Banner

ALLIES: Power Man,
Spider-Man, Iron Fist

FOES: The Leader, the
Abomination, Rhino

STRENGTHS: Almost
invulnerable, super-strong,
swift healing powers, can
resist mind control,
amazing jumping power

WEAKNESS:
Getting very cross!

RICK'S ROLES
Banner is blasted by the
gamma bomb and becomes
Hulk, but he saves **teenager
Rick Jones** from the same
fate! Rick has since been:

- **Hulk's friend**
- **Hulk's boss**
- A mega-strong
  Rick Jones-Hulk
- A blue monster
  called **A-Bomb**
- A best-selling
  novelist!

BAD DAY

Childlike and lonely,
Savage Hulk tries to
**"make friends with the
stars"**. He leaps into
orbit, faints from **lack
of oxygen** – and **comes
down to Earth** with a
massive crash!

HRH THE HULK!
After crash-landing on the
planet Sakaar, the Hulk is
forced to fight as a gladiator
by its wicked ruler, the Red
King. The Hulk leads a
rebellion against him, and
is crowned king!

BIG TROUBLE!

A massive dose of **gamma rays** from an
experimental bomb changes the **DNA** of
scientist **Dr. Bruce Banner**. Now, whenever
he is overwhelmed by **anger** or **fear**,
Banner transforms into a **rampaging,
green-skinned giant** – the **Incredible Hulk!**

150,000,000,000

The weight in tons of the mountain range Molecule Man drops on the Hulk! The Hulk catches it—proving he's an unbelievable powerhouse!

BETWEEN...

The Hulk's skin was grey in his very first appearance in *Incredible Hulk #1* (May 1962). The colour was hard to print correctly – so in the next issue he became "ol' greenskin"!

...THE PANELS

HULKING LINE UP

We measure up the various incarnations of the Hulk!

Bruce Banner 1.8m (5ft 9½in), 58kg (128lbs)

Gray Hulk 1.98m (6ft 6in), 408kg (900 lbs)

Green Hulk 2.4m (8ft), 635kg (1,400lbs)

MEGA MAKEOVER
The Himalayan nation of Llhasa is under threat from General Fang's armies. Hulk dresses up in a fur suit against the cold and puts Fang's armies to flight. They think he's the yeti!

TOP 5

Hulk Incarnations

There have been a whole lotta Hulks! Here are just a few:

1 SAVAGE HULK – big, green and childlike – unless he gets scared or angry.

2 'JOE FIXIT' – grey, mean and cunning; a notorious Las Vegas gangster!

3 WORLD BREAKER – when the Hulk gets really, really angry!

4 DOC GREEN – Banner uses Extremis nanobots to repair his brain. Hulk becomes both big and brilliant!

5 SAVAGE BANNER – the Savage Hulk's mind, in Banner's body. Not very scary, to be honest!

TEAM PLAYERS

Super-shrink Doc Samson **separates** Bruce Banner from the Hulk. Banner then forms a team of **Hulkbusters** to **take down** Hulk!

REALLY?!

When Loki frames the Hulk for attacking a train, the bewildered behemoth **disguises** himself as a **robot** and gets a job **juggling animals** in a **circus**! The Avengers' first mission is to find him.

KAPOW!

Hulk can cause a **sonic boom** by **clapping his hands** – and knock enemies **off their feet!**

NOT A SCRATCH!
The Hulk really is super-tough. In one single battle he is shot with:

• a napalm rocket launcher

• an elephant gun

• an anthrax grenade launcher

• a shotgun firing 40,000,000-volt taser rounds

He never even blinks!

MAESTRO HULK
100 years in the future, Earth is devastated by nuclear war. Hulk is **driven mad** by radiation and turns into the **Maestro** – an **evil, bearded overlord!**

TRUE LOVE
Jarella, princess of the subatomic kingdom of K'ai, loves **both** Bruce Banner **and** the Hulk! She could have been **the one**, but tragically she dies...

WHO'S THE DADDY?

For a long time, twins **Wanda** and **Pietro** believe that **Magneto** is their father! They eventually discover that their true parents are Romany travelers from Transia. The twins' mutant powers are the results of genetic experiments by scientist the **High Evolutionary** and his god-like power.

 TELL ME MORE!

Wanda already has the potential to become an energy-manipulating mutant. However, the demonic Elder God Chthon then imbues her with magical abilities as well.

Power Up!

A WITCH IN TRAINING

To help control her powers, the witch **AGATHA HARKNESS** tutors Wanda in the art of sorcery. Magical knowledge combined with her superhuman abilities increases Wanda's power, but things **STILL GO WRONG!**

HEX POWER!

The Scarlet Witch can **reshape reality,** giving her **immense power.** You might think that would make her happy, but Wanda is a **complex soul** – unsure of **who her parents are,** troubled about her **lost children** and vulnerable to **villainous manipulations.**

FAST FACTS

FULL NAME:
Wanda Maximoff

STRENGTHS: Mutant Hex power alters reality; sorcery training to control magical powers

WEAKNESSES: Influence of villains such as Doctor Doom can lead to destructive urges; training only 80 per cent effective

ALLIES: Vision, Quicksilver, Avengers, Wonder Man, Agatha Harkness

FOES: Doctor Doom, Chthon, Mephisto, Master Pandemonium

LOVE TRIANGLE

Scarlet Witch marries the android **Vision**, who is programmed with the brainwaves of dead hero **Wonder Man**. When Vision's programming is wiped and Wonder Man **returns from the grave**, Wanda starts dating him instead!

 Yesss!! Scarlet Witch becomes such a **powerful sorcerer** that she even manages to defeat the dread demon **Dormammu**.

DIVIDED LOYALTIES

Magneto saves young Wanda and her brother **Pietro** (Quicksilver) from a mob. They join his **Brotherhood of Evil** Mutants, battling the X-Men, but their hearts aren't in it and they join Captain America's new Avengers team instead.

Demon Doll

The demon **Chthon** tries to use the Scarlet Witch as a vessel for his **demonic doings.** The Avengers trap his **essence** in a **doll**, and the Scarlet Witch buries the doll beneath an **avalanche**. But you can't keep a demon like Chthon down **for long...**

TEAM PLAYER

Scarlet Witch becomes leader of Super Hero team Force Works. Her Hex mainframe computer predicts in advance where trouble is most likely to flare up.

REALLY?!

Scarlet Witch loses her powers and memory and **almost marries Doctor Doom!** Iron Lad and the Young Avengers rescue her and they all travel back in time. Wanda gets her powers back, tries to **undo** the past harm she's done and repower all mutants. Then Doctor Doom **steals her powers!**

"There is no defense against the Scarlet Witch's *HEX!*"

TOP 3

Wanda Weird-Outs

1 Wanda has twin sons with her then-husband Vision. When they vanish, she goes mad, blames the Avengers, destroys Avengers Mansion and kills several teammates, including Vision and Ant-Man (Scott Lang).

2 Wanda reshapes reality so that mutants rule, with Magneto in charge.

3 Wanda changes reality again so that most mutants are depowered.

PS: DOCTOR DOOM WAS REALLY TO BLAME!

AAARRGHH!!

Scarlet Witch doesn't know how powerful she is. She's **RESHAPED** reality, **CREATED** life, **DEPOWERED** heroes and brought friends **BACK TO LIFE!** Who knows what she'll do next!

WORLD SAVIOUR

The cosmic Phoenix Force possesses some of the X-Men, driving them on to rule the world. Scarlet Witch rejoins the Avengers to help expel the destructive Phoenix Force from Earth.

A HAPPY ENDING?

Wanda is a "Nexus Being" – a living focal point for Earth's mystical energies. Her power, combined with that of Doctor Doom, captures the Life Force and gives her back her sons, Wiccan and Speed.

BORN TO RUN

Blink and you'll **miss** these **lightning-quick** speedsters. Whether they're on the run from the law or **chasing fast-fleeing felons,** these super-powered sprinters know how to **finish first!** Catch 'em if you can!

BETWEEN...

The super-fast amnesiac calling himself "Buried Alien" is a nod to DC Comics' The Flash (Barry Allen). Could The Flash have run so fast, he'd been transported to the Marvel Universe?

...THE PANELS

TOP 4
Super-Fast Feats

1 **QUICKSILVER** – sprints from Tibet to Indonesia in just a few seconds!

2 **SURGE** – runs from New York to Colorado in an afternoon!

3 **MAKKARI** – makes cyclones by running around in circles!

4 **SPEED DEMON** – runs straight up walls and across water!

REALLY?!

World War II hero the **Whizzer** obtains incredible **super speed** after being injected with the **blood of a Mongoose!**

"I'm freaking *QUICKSILVER!!!* and you can eat my freaking *DUST!*"

Speed

Quicksilver

Speed Demon

Rocket Raccoon

48

ALTERNATE UNIVERSE

In the Marvel Zombies universe (Earth-2149), Quicksilver's extreme speed spreads the zombie virus across the globe like wildfire!

Natural Velocity
New Warrior **Speedball** is super-fast, but doesn't have super-speed! He uses **kinetic force fields** to travel at extreme velocities by **bouncing off** solid objects.

WOW!

12,250

Quicksilver's top speed in kph (7,612mph).

Power Up!

GODLY GALLOPER
Quicksilver loses his powers, exposing himself to the Inhumans' gene-altering Terrigen Mist crystals. He briefly gains the ability to leap through time!

Q: How does Spitfire get her powers?

A: British MI-13 agent Lady Jacqueline Falsworth receives **a blood transfusion** from android the Human Torch, but with a side effect – she gains **super-speed!**

Makkari

NOoooo!!

Light-speed lowlife **SPEEDFREEK** is battling the **NEW WARRIORS** when his partner, **NITRO THE LIVING BOMB,** destroys a school, sparking the superhuman civil war!

YESSS!

Quicksilver is so fast, he can attack opponents from multiple angles in a split second, and dodge anything they throw at him—he can even outrun Thor's lightning bolts!

SPACE RACE

Elder of the Universe the **Runner** invites **Quicksilver, Makkari, Black Racer, Captain Marvel, Speed Demon, Super Sabre** and **Whizzer** to take part in a race to prove who is Earth's fastest. Makkari sets the pace, but the mysterious **"Buried Alien"** comes from nowhere to win!

WHO'S FASTEST?

ON YOUR MARKS...

ROCKET RACCOON: He might have a powerful brain, but he only has little raccoon legs!

SPEED DEMON: This fleet-footed felon will do anything to cross the line first!

SPEED: No matter what he says, this kid is not overtaking Quicksilver!

QUICKSILVER: Once Pietro Maximoff is in the lead, surely no one is catching the ultimate super-sprinter!

MAKKARI: It takes something special to slip past this Eternal speedster!

WOW!

10,000+

The number of lives Spidey has probably saved.

COMES GREAT
RESPONSIBILITY

WEBSWINGER!

Debuting in 1962, Spider-Man was a new kind of hero – a teenager fans could easily identify with. As writer Stan Lee says in *The Amazing Spider-Man #9*, Spider-Man is "the Super Hero who could be—you!"

...THE PANELS

Q: How does Spider-Man create his webs?

A: Peter Parker can **climb like a spider,** but most of the time he isn't able to shoot **spider silk** naturally. Parker invents **web-shooters,** worn on both wrists and fuelled by **web fluid.**

He's your friendly neighbourhood Spider-Man, the **Wallcrawler,** the **Webswinger,** the Webhead. These are all names for the secret ID of Peter Parker, a shy student **transformed** into an amazing Super Hero by the **bite of a spider!**

NOOOOO!!

Spidey loses his powers when he comes down **WITH A COLD!** He's unmasked by Doc Ock, but no one believes **PUNY PETER** could really be Spider-Man!

HELLO MARY JANE!

"Face it tiger, you just hit the jackpot!"—Mary Jane first meets Peter on a blind date arranged for him by Aunt May. And so begins Peter and MJ's long, on-off romance. At one point they even get married!

S.H.I.E.L.D. DECLASSIFIED

DAWN OF THE SPIDER-MAN
After his parents are killed in a plane crash, Peter Parker is raised by his Aunt May and Uncle Ben. A radioactive spider-bite gives Peter incredible powers, and he becomes a TV star. Everything changes when a criminal kills Uncle Ben! Peter blames himself and vows to use his powers to protect the innocent from now on.

ALTERNATE UNIVERSE

Spider-Monkey (Peter Parker) is a "webswinger" from Earth-8101. The friendly neighbourhood primate joins the spider-army of Spider-Man – who is Otto Octavius!

"My **SPIDER-SENSE** is tingling."

DASTARDLY DEED!

Chameleon and Green Goblin try to drive Spidey crazy by using **androids** to impersonate Mary and Richard Parker, Peter's dead **mum and dad!**

TELL ME MORE!

Peter Parker's spider-sense gives him a tingling sensation at the base of his skull when danger is near. This instinct also helps him swing across New York City, without even having to look where he's going!

REALLY?!

When Spider-Man loses his costume, **Johnny Storm** loans him a Fantastic Four uniform and a **brown paper bag** for a mask. The bag says **"Kick Me"** on the back!

TOP 3

Spider-Men

1 SPIDERY SPIDER-MAN – Peter is kissed by the Spider-Queen (Adriana Soria) and is transformed into a full-on spider by her mutagenic enzymes!

2 SPIDER-HULK – Spidey is zapped with a biokinetic energy ray while battling the Hulk. He absorbs the Hulk's energy and turns big and green!

3 SIX-ARMED SPIDER-MAN – Peter experiments with a formula to restore him to normal (without spider powers), and grows four extra arms!

A DEAL WITH A DEMON!

To save **Aunt May** from death, Peter makes **a deal** with the **demon Mephisto**. The demon **re-arranges history**, saving Aunt May's life, but Peter's marriage to Mary Jane is also **wiped from reality!**

BETWEEN...

Stan Lee has joked that J. Jonah Jameson, fiery Editor-in-Chief of the *Daily Bugle*, New York City mayor and chief thorn-in-the-side of Spider-Man, is actually based on himself!

...THE PANELS

FAST FACTS

REAL NAME: Peter Benjamin Parker

BASE: New York City

STRENGTHS: Highly-intelligent; proportional reflexes; spider powers; spider-sense; generates web with web-shooters

WEAKNESSES: Enemies exploit his love of friends and family; vulnerable to power loss

FOES: Norman Osborn (Green Goblin), Doctor Octopus, Vulture, Electro, Jackal, Kingpin

ALLIES: Fantastic Four, Avengers, X-Men, Black Cat, Daredevil, Firestar

53

FAST FACTS

REAL NAME:
Jessica Miriam Drew

STRENGTHS: Spider powers, energy blasts, mood-altering pheromones, flight, resists poisons

WEAKNESSES: Prone to losing powers, hates rats

FOES: Hydra, Morgan le Fay, Charlotte Witter

FAST WORK
In London, Jessica evades capture by a Scotland Yard detective by ripping up a lamppost and **throwing it at him!** To stop it from killing him, she then zooms in front of her own projectile and pushes him **out of the way!**

"From now on Spider-Woman FIGHTS BACK!"

Q: Is Spider-Woman related to Spider-Man?

A: Only through the web of life! Jessica Drew's origins have nothing to do with Peter Parker's radioactive spider bite.

WHEN GOOD GUYS

...AND GOOD AGAIN!
When Spider-Woman loses her powers, a Hydra agent promises to restore them if she joins S.H.I.E.L.D. as a double agent. Spymaster Nick Fury encourages her to take the deal – and topple Hydra from within!

KAPOW!
Jessica's body naturally produces **bio-electrical energy**, which she channels into a powerful **"venom blast"**.

ID PARADE
There's been more than one Spider-Woman...

Super Hero special agent and Avenger.

Former government agent, now powerful psychic Madame Web.

Spider-human hybrid controlled by Doctor Octopus to attack other Spider-Women, gain their powers, kill Spider-Man.

Teenager who defeats Charlotte Witter.

JESSICA DREW

JULIA CARPENTER

CHARLOTTE WITTER

MATTIE FRANKLIN

SPECIAL AGENT SPIDER
Spider-Woman is a seasoned secret agent, going deep undercover for S.H.I.E.L.D., tracking down alien threats for S.W.O.R.D. and serving on the Secret Avengers team alongside ex-boyfriend Hawkeye, espionage expert Black Widow and mad scientist M.O.D.O.K.!

REALLY?!

During a Super Villain prison break, Spider-Woman joins the New Avengers. But she's no hero – she's the **Skrull Queen Veranke!** The shape-shifting Queen is planning a **secret invasion of Earth!**

SPIDER SCIENCE!

Spider-Man isn't the **only** wall-crawler in town! Jessica Drew certainly hasn't had an easy life, but she chooses to protect ordinary folks as the Super Hero **Spider-Woman!**

AAARRGHH!!

Jessica's hand-to-hand skills come from her time with **TERRORIST ORGANISATION HYDRA**. It takes years for Jessica to shake the **FALSE MEMORIES** Hydra uses to control her.

Magical mayhem

Spider-Woman has made a frequent enemy of legendary sorceress **Morgan le Fay** – even travelling back through time to clash with the wicked magician!

ALTERNATE UNIVERSE

The Jessica Drew of the Ultimate Universe is actually an **altered clone** of Peter Parker, alias Spider-Man!

BETWEEN...

A pregnant Jessica stars on the cover of *Spider-Woman #1* (November 2015). The Marvel team wanted to explore her success in combining the roles of Super Hero sleuth and mother-to-be!

...THE PANELS

TELL ME MORE!

Jessica's scientist parents, Jonathan and Miriam Drew, are seeking to "improve" human DNA with spider abilities. When Jessica falls gravely ill, Jonathan gives her experimental injections of their spider serum to save her life, and she gains super-spider powers.

BY THE SERAPHIM'S SILENT CHANT... AND BY MUNNOPOR'S MYSTIC MOON... MAY OMNISCIENT OSHTUR GRANT... THIS FATEFUL BOON!

TEAM PLAYER

Dr Strange forms the heroic Defenders, a team with no official roster or charter, to guard Earth from intergalactic and supernatural threats.

Q: How does Doctor Strange learn magic?

A: Stephen Strange is a brilliant, but arrogant, surgeon – until he **injures his hands.** Desperate to find a cure, he tracks down legendary mystic the **Ancient One** in the Himalayas. The Ancient One is Earth's **Sorcerer Supreme** and he chooses Strange as his apprentice!

FAST FACTS

REAL NAME:
Dr Stephen Vincent Strange

ALIASES: Sorcerer Supreme, Master of the Mystic Arts

STRENGTHS: A hugely powerful magician, with a library of spells and a collection of magical artefacts

WEAKNESSES: Limited fighting ability and strength (he's only human)

ALLIES: Avengers, Defenders, Clea

FOES: Baron Mordo, Dormammu, Shuma-Gorath, Nightmare

CLOAK OF LEVITATION

Want to fly? This cloak is what you need! It obeys Doctor Strange's commands, even when he's not wearing it!

WHEN GOOD GUYS GO BAD!

ENTER THE RED RAJAH!

A magical ruby known as the Star of Capistan takes control of Doctor Strange! He becomes the Red Rajah and tries to magically brainwash everyone in Manhattan!

REALLY?!

Doctor Strange often battles **occult threats,** but he also manages to save Earth from a **Skrull invasion fleet.** Using the **Images of Ikonn** spell, he creates a **huge illusion** of **Galactus** that sends the aliens packing!

FACE THE STRANGE!

Doctor Strange is famous for his **disco stage-magician look,** but when the demon **Asmodeus** steals his appearance, Strange **revamps his style** with a skintight outfit, Super Hero-style hood and chest symbol!

STRANGE MAGIC

Doctor Strange is the **Sorcerer Supreme**, Earth's mightiest magician. Other heroes battle Super Villains and alien invaders – Strange **protects** our planet from **demons, warlocks** and **spooky entities** from **mystic dimensions!**

"Where mankind is **MENACED** by magic... there must Dr. Strange go to **COMBAT** it!"

S.H.I.E.L.D. DECLASSIFIED

THE SANCTUM SANTORUM
Doctor Strange's home – his Sanctum Sanctorum – houses his collection of magical items and books and is protected by powerful enchantments. It stands on a place of mystical power in New York's Greenwich Village.

Astral Travel!
One of the **mystic arts** Doctor Strange has mastered is **astral travel** – his spirit can leave his body and **travel unseen** across the world.

Weakness:
His astral form can be **seen by spirits** (and the Hulk!), and his **body is helpless** while his spirit is away!

BETWEEN...

How did Doctor Strange get his name? His adventures first appeared in *Strange Tales* (beginning #110, July 1963), so creator Steve Ditko named him after the comic!

...THE PANELS

TELL ME MORE!

Doctor Strange receives spells, magical items and help from three ancient godlike beings named the Vishanti. They are Oshtur the Omnipotent, Agamotto the All-Seeing and Hoary Hoggoth.

AAAARRGHH!!!
Dr Strange's brother, **VICTOR**, dies. Trying to revive him, Strange uses a spell from the evil **VAMPIRIC VERSES**. Vic returns as troubled vampire hero **BARON BLOOD.**

Q: Who is Wong?

A: He's Doctor Strange's **manservant**, equally handy at martial arts, magic **and cooking!** He's been Strange's faithful servant for years, despite being scarred, kidnapped and even **turned into a vampire!**

TOP 5

Strange Spells!

1 IMAGES OF IKONN
A powerful illusion spell that has even terrified the mighty Galactus!
[USEFULNESS: 10/10]

2 CRIMSON BANDS OF CYTTORAK These glowing magic ribbons can even imprison the Hulk!
USEFULNESS: 9/10

3 THE SEVEN RINGS OF RAGGADOR Blue energy rings that protect Doctor Strange from harm!
USEFULNESS: 7/10

4 WINDS OF WATOOMB
This whirlwind can whisk Strange across the world – or blow enemies away!
USEFULNESS: 7/10

5 FLAMES OF THE FALTINE
These green fiery bolts strike fear into foes!
USEFULNESS: 6/10

SUPERNATURAL!

These **spooky sorts** really put the "**super**" into "**supernatural**"! They come from **mystical dimensions**; they possess powers **beyond human understanding** and, if you're not careful, **they're coming after you**!

> "I am the spirit of **VENGEANCE. NOTHING** will stop me..."

NEED HELP?!
Looking for a **hero** to battle a supernatural threat? If **Doctor Strange** is busy, try **Doctor Voodoo**, who has also held the title of **Sorcerer Supreme**!

VAMPIRE HERO
BLADE'S mother is bitten while giving birth, giving Blade **IMMUNITY** to full vampirism. He becomes a Daywalker – a vampire who is impervious to sunlight. Blade battles vampire villains, like Dracula.

FAST FACTS

SUPERNATURAL SAVIOURS: Ghost Rider, Blade, Caretaker, Werewolf By Night

FEARSOME FOES: Dracula, Nightmare, Blackheart, Master Pandemonium, Satannish

SOMEWHERE IN BETWEEN: Daimon Hellstrom

PARTY ANIMAL!
Jack Russell is a normal(ish) teenager – until he turns into the **Werewolf By Night**. A pity it has to happen in the middle of his **18th** birthday party!

DEMON HOST
Master Pandemonium's limbs have been **replaced by demons**, granting him command of **dark forces**. He also controls the **Rakasha**, a horde of demons that actually live in his body!

FRIGHT NIGHT

Nightmare is the demon lord of a dream dimension. He haunts the sleeping minds of wicked humans upon his horse **Dreamstalker**. If Nightmare has his way, all humanity will fall into an eternal slumber full of frights!

Ghost Riders have the ability to manifest and control **hellfire-infused chains**, often with sharp **hooks** and **sickles** attached.

A Ghost Rider's greatest weapon is his **Penance Stare**, an **incapacitating** gaze that forces his enemy to experience every **pain** he or she has ever inflicted on an **innocent** person.

Q: Daimon Hellstrom: hero or villain?

A: A bit of both! The **Son of Satan** looks down on mere mortals. When it suits him, he allies with **heroes** like the **Defenders**. And when a wicked mood strikes? He hangs with Baron Zemo as a **Master of Evil!**

WHAT?!

There have been **many** Ghost Riders and some **don't use** motorcycles. Transport includes a **hot rod**, a **horse**, a **bear** and even a **shark!**

AAARRGHH!!

DRACULA, Lord of the Vampires, makes a deal with DOCTOR DOOM, and tries to turn the U.K. into a VAMPIRE STATE!!

YECCH!

Satannish is an immensely powerful demonic being who most often appears to humans as a **green-skinned, horned monstrosity with a second, toothy face in his stomach!**

WEIRD AND WONDERFUL

When **the world** is swarming with **mutating mists** and portals to **bizarre realities,** things are bound to get a little... strange. From **amphibian thunder gods,** to a Super Hero **alien duck,** let's meet the oddest dwellers in the universe!

> "I've become something greater than either *SPIDER* or *PIG*... I've become a *SPIDER-HAM!*"

REALLY?!

Spider-Ham is a **mild-mannered spider** who is bitten by a **radioactive pig.** He turns into an **anthropomorphic** (humanlike) **porker!**

Living **cartoon hero** Slapstick is an honorary **New Warrior.** He'll **mash** you with his **mallet** if you insult his teen teammates!

TOP 5

Spider-Ham's Enemies

1 **BULLFROG** – humanoid, thieving frog.

2 **BUZZARD** – humanoid, con-man possum.

3 **KINGPIG** – humanoid, porcine crime boss.

4 **RAVEN THE HUNTER** – humanoid, big-game-hunting raven.

5 **HOGZILLA** – a giant, reptilian pig!

BUZZWORTHY

Scientist Fritz von Meyer's attempt to control a **mutated bee colony** backfires when the insects **devour** him... but his consciousness **lives on** through **Swarm** – a **sentient mass** of living bees.

AAAARRGHH!!

The first time Swarm **CLASHES** with Spider-Man, the webslinger gets him to **BUZZ OFF** by coating his spider-suit in **BUG SPRAY!**

WEIRD WILDLIFE

HOWARD THE DUCK
Born on planet Duckworld, where intelligent life evolved from waterfowl.

PET AVENGERS
Team of furry, feathered and fanged Super Hero animals.

SQUIRREL GIRL
Part-human, part-squirrel mutant, aka Dorothy Green.

HOW TO MAKE A DRAMATIC ENTRANCE BY HOWARD THE DUCK

Get stolen from your home planet by wicked Thog the Overmaster.

↓

Fall to Earth.

↓

Encounter the monstrous swamp beast, Man-Thing.

↓

Get attacked by Bessie the Vampire Cow.

Squirrel Girl's best friend, **Tippy-Toe** the squirrel, is much cleverer than the average rodent. Tippy-Toe not only helps defeat Super Villain **M.O.D.O.K.**, she can use the Great Lakes Avengers' **blender** to make herself **acorn smoothies!**

YESSS!

Squirrel Girl doesn't just talk to squirrels! She's defeated **Doctor Doom, Fin Fang Foom, Bi-Beast** and even **persuaded** Galactus not to **devour the Earth!**

Q: Does Howard the Duck have superpowers?

A: As well as some talent for magic, Howard is a master of the **ancient martial art** of **Quack-Fu**.

TEAM PLAYERS

Howard teams up with beautiful model **Beverly Switzler** to fight foes like **Turnip Man, Count Macho** and the gigantic **Gingerbread Man!**

ALTERNATE UNIVERSE

Moon Boy is a **small, furry humanoid** with an unusual best buddy – a **bright red T-Rex** named Devil Dinosaur! Moon Boy rescued him as a **baby** on their primitive home planet of **Dinosaur World.**

Can't touch this!

The Man-Thing's **semiliquid** body is made of **roots** and **slime**. It is almost **indestructible** – so foes who try to hurt him with hammers, pickaxes and laser pistols will be **disappointed!**

FREE ACORNS

SUPER VILLAINS

FAMILY CONNECTIONS

Thanos has **big family problems!** His brother **Starfox** helps the Avengers defeat him, his adopted daughters **Moondragon** and **Gamora** reject him, his granddaughter **Nebula** steals his Infinity Gauntlet and he tries to kill **Thane**, his only son! Even **Thanos's mother** tries to kill him, so he **returns the favour!**

MOMMY

"...Interesting."
Thanos's last word when he realises that Drax the Destroyer has punched through his chest and taken out his heart!

TITAN OF TERROR

Thanos is a threat to **every living thing** in the **universe!** The mad Titan is obsessed with **conquering worlds** in order to inflict immeasurable **death and destruction!**

ENERGY DIET

Thanos does not need to eat or drink. He can get by on ambient cosmic energy alone.

BACK FROM THE DEAD!

Thanos has been turned to stone, suspended in amber and **Drax** has even removed his heart. Then **Death** resurrects him – and he becomes **almost invincible!**

TOP 5

Thanos's Gadgets

1 **FORCE FIELD GENERATOR** – to protect against projectiles

2 **ROBOT DRONES** – minions to perform any number of jobs

3 **TIME PROBE** – time machine for complicated schemes

4 **FLYING SPACE THRONE** – for teleportation and inter-dimensional travel

5 **THE SANCTUARY** – mobile space station

S.H.I.E.L.D. DECLASSIFIED

THE INFINITY GAUNTLET
The Infinity Gauntlet gives power over time, space and reality itself. Thanos's tremendous strength and psychic powers, together with this cosmic artefact, make him almost unstoppable.

TEAM PLAYER

In his quest for the **Infinity Gems**, Thanos forms the **Black Order**, a group of deadly aliens, to help him **conquer** and **destroy** worlds.

HANDLE WITH CARE!

Thanos absorbs the power of the **Cosmic Cube,** then discards it. Wrong move! The Cube still has some power left – and **Captain Mar-Vell** uses it to defeat him!

GRUDGE MATCH

Few can take on **the mad Titan** and win, but he meets his match in **Drax the Destroyer.** Drax is a genetically engineered being with one purpose – **to destroy Thanos!**

BEFORE...

AFTER...

Thanos spends his youth **madly in love** with a woman he meets on Titan, and he destroys **countless worlds** to impress her. The mystery woman reveals herself as **Death** in disguise, but Thanos **still loves her!**

"Let the universe cower in *FEAR!*"

Two of a Kind

Thanos is in love with Death, but she doesn't feel the same way. He seeks the Infinity Gems just so he can cause as much destruction as possible – and finally make her happy!

WOW!

100,000,000

The estimated number of people that Thanos has killed – but the total could be even higher!

FAST FACTS

RACE: Mutated Eternal (a race of genetically altered humans)

HOMEWORLD: Saturn's moon, Titan

STRENGTHS: Telepathy, energy projection, super strength, intelligence – he can do almost anything!

WEAKNESSES: He's so evil, the whole universe wants to defeat him!

ALLIES: Death

FOES: Guardians of the Galaxy, Drax the Destroyer, Avengers, Adam Warlock

> **AAAARRGHH!!**
> When **ODIN** creates the **DESTROYER** armour to save humanity from some future foe, he doesn't expect Loki to steal its **POWER** and use it against **THOR!**

GOOD DAY
Loki turns a **tree** into a **tiger** to attack Thor's girlfriend Jane Foster, puts a **force field** around **Mjolnir** (so Thor can't use it), makes **people disappear**, turns New York City into **ice cream** and stops **an atomic bomb** exploding – all in one day!

MISCHIEF MAKER!

Loki is the shape-shifting **God of Mischief** – one of the **greatest sorcerers** in all of Asgard. With this **trickster,** you can be sure of just one thing – he's out for **number one!**

BETWEEN...
Loki first stirred up trouble in August 1949 as the main villain of *Venus* #6, a fantasy romance comic book about the Earthly adventures of the goddess of love.

...THE PANELS

BEFORE...
Loki is a master of magic and illusion, and he has taken on many forms, including several versions of himself. These include Kid Loki, Young Loki – even Lady Loki!

Kid Loki

Young Loki

Lady Loki

AFTER...

TELL ME MORE!
Prophecies link Loki to Ragnarok – the Norse word for the end of everything. As well as trying to overthrow his adoptive father, Odin, and tormenting his brother, Thor, Loki also nearly destroys Asgard many times over!

REALLY?!
Loki can even trick **himself!** Kid Loki traps his older, more evil self within a **magpie** called **Ikol.**

FAST FACTS
REAL NAME: Loki Laufeyson

STRENGTHS: Cunning, sorcery, astral projection, shape-shifting, inter-dimensional travel

WEAKNESSES: Lust for power, too clever by half – nobody likes a wiseguy!

FOES: Anyone who stands in his way – often Thor and the Avengers

DREAM JOB: Supreme ruler of Asgard

Q: Why does Loki hate his adoptive father, Odin?

A: Loki cannot forgive Odin for killing his **Frost Giant father, Laufey** – even though Laufey **abandoned Loki as a baby!**

"The Age of Odin and his sons is ending... Fire and chaos are coming. *AND I AM THE LORD OF CHAOS!*"

BEST KNOWN FOR

TORMENTING HIS BROTHER, THOR, AND TRYING TO DESTROY ASGARD!

Old West outlaw

Teenage trickster

YESSS!!

LOKI uses an illusion to keep the **FIRE DEMON SURTUR** at bay until his brother, **THOR**, and his father, **ODIN**, can join him and **SAVE ASGARD!**

50

The weight in tons that Loki can lift.

WHEN BAD GUYS GO GOOD!

LOKI THE WORTHY
To stop the Red Skull, Scarlet Witch and Doctor Strange cast an inversion spell – turning bad guys good! Loki gets so good, he's worthy to wield Thor's hammer, Mjolnir!

Worthy to wield Thor's hammer

FAST FACTS

REAL NAME:
Nathaniel Richards

STRENGTHS: Futuristic battle armour, high intelligence, skill with technology, combat expertise, political manipulation, slowed aging

WEAPONS: Battle armour fires energy blasts, provides super-strength, enhanced durability; can summon any weapon from the timestream with a finger-snap

FOES: Fantastic Four, Avengers

TOP 7 ITEMS IN KANG'S TROPHY ROOM

CAPTAIN AMERICA'S SHIELDS

THOR'S MJOLNIR

DOCTOR OCTOPUS'S TENTACLES

ULTRON

SILVER SURFER'S SURFBOARD

MAGNETO'S HELMET

WOLVERINE'S ADAMANTIUM SKELETON

IDENTITY CRISIS!

Too many Kangs spoil the timestream! Travelling through time creates loads of alternate Kangs, so Prime Kang sets out with two other Kangs to remove all the others from existence!

S.H.I.E.L.D. DECLASSIFIED

CUNNING OPERATOR
When Kang heads to a new time, he takes on a new persona and blends in well with that era's society and culture. He politically manoeuvres or aggressively attacks, with one aim – to conquer!

REALLY?!

Kang **changes his own timeline** to remove being bullied as a child. Young Nathaniel, seeing Kang as his **villainous fate,** joins the Young Avengers as **Iron Lad!** But after the death of his friend **Cassandra Lang,** he changes into the evil **Kid Immortus!**

"All of *HISTORY* is my weapon... I fight with *TIME* itself. You are its *PLAYTHINGS.* I am its *CONQUEROR.*"

7,000
The span of years that Kang travels – from Ancient Egypt to the year 4,000. He may journey even farther!

TIME-TRAVELLING TYRANT

Born on an **alternative Earth** in the year 3000, Super Villain **Kang** rebuilds Doctor Doom's old **time machine** with one purpose: to conquer all of **space and time!**

TOP 4
Kang Characters

1 PHARAOH RAMA-TUT – uses future technology to conquer Ancient Egypt and tries to make Invisible Woman his queen!

2 VICTOR TIMELY – mayor of Timely in 20th-century Illinois. Tries to destroy the Avengers with a robotic Spider-Man.

3 THE SCARLET CENTURION – tricks the Avengers into hunting Super Heroes and Villains for him!

4 IMMORTUS – a possible future version of Kang seeking mastery over all of time.

BEST KNOWN FOR
CONQUERING, TIME TRAVEL AND HIS BLUE FACE

Kang wants to marry **Princess Ravonna Redslayer** and add her kingdom to his empire, but she declines. Kang refuses to execute the princess, so his furious army kidnaps her! Kang teams up with the Avengers to rescue his lady love.

PRINCE CHARMING ➤

AAARRGHH!!
Kang kidnaps the **APOCALYPSE TWINS**, raising the pair with the aim of using them to resurrect the **FOUR HORSEMEN OF DEATH** and cause the **END OF EVERYTHING!**

Q: Why is Kang's face blue?
A: Kang's technologically advanced battle armour makes it *look* like his face is blue! Actually, he is a normal human being from the future.

FAMILY CONNECTIONS
Kang is rumoured to be a distant descendant of **Reed Richards** (Mister Fantastic) and possibly of the scientist and sorcerer **Doctor Doom.**

4

The number of times Skull's body is destroyed, only for him to return!

SIN

The Red Skull steals **Professor X's body** and grafts a piece of the **X-Men leader's brain** into his own brain to gain some of the prof's **psychic powers!**

TELL ME MORE!

Adolf Hitler personally manages the training of Johann Shmidt to turn him into the "perfect Nazi". He gives him a hideous red skull mask and, as the Red Skull, Shmidt becomes the Third Reich's secret second-in-command, carrying out Hitler's most evil missions!

FAMILY CONNECTIONS

The Red Skull brings up his daughter, **Sin,** to be a **killing machine.** As a test, he pits her in combat against **Baron Zemo,** planning to choose the victor **as his heir.** Although Sin seemingly **kills the Baron,** the Red Skull **rejects her...** but she soon **claims his mantle!**

Crossbones and **Sin** help the Red Skull assassinate Captain America after the superhuman civil war. **The Winter Soldier** captures Crossbones, but **Sin escapes** – and stabs Cap's beloved, **Sharon Carter!**

FAST FACTS

REAL NAME: Johann Shmidt

HOME NATION: Germany

STRENGTHS: High intelligence, master military strategist, master of disguise, skilled unarmed combatant and marksman

WEAKNESSES: He's too evil! A lot of Super Villains refuse to ally with Skull because he's a Nazi

ALLIES: Adolf Hitler, Arnim Zola, Crossbones, Doctor Faustus, Hydra, Sin

FOES: Captain America, Avengers, the Winter Soldier

S.H.I.E.L.D. DECLASSIFIED

SKULL AND CROSSBONES
Young neo-Nazi Brock Rumlow dreams of working for his hero, the Red Skull. This comes true when, as Crossbones, he is recruited as Skull's main henchman. Crossbones is an expert martial artist and marksman; he also briefly gains the power to shoot blasts of fire from his face.

FACE OF EVIL

The **Red Skull** is one of the most evil men in history. He **changes his form** and his identity. He's defeated. **He's even killed.** But he always returns with another **dastardly plot!**

> "And now a toast...to **UNENDING CONQUEST!**"

BAD TO THE BONE

The Red Skull is so nasty that even Adolf Hitler is scared of him!

BACK WITH A BANG

After **decades in hibernation,** the Red Skull is revived by **A.I.M.,** but he steals their **Cosmic Cube!** This gives him the power to **change reality.** Luckily, he doesn't have it for long!

CAUGHT IN TWO MINDS

K.G.B. General **Aleksander Lukin** shoots the Red Skull to steal his **Cosmic Cube.** Skull's body dies, but he uses the Cube to trap their minds together – **inside Lukin's body!**

THE DUST OF DEATH

Skull's personal chemical weapon kills on contact with the skin – but not before the victim's head tightens and shrivels into a bright red skull!

TOP 3

Skull Subordinates

1 **ARNIM ZOLA** – Hitler's personal physician, the man responsible for the Red Skull's frequent body changes.

2 **CROSSBONES (BROCK RUMLOW)** – the Red Skull's head henchman

3 **SIN (SINTHEA SHMIDT)** – Skull's evil daughter and heir.

Osborn's business partner, Prof Mendel Stromm, discovers a formula to enhance human strength. Osborn frames Stromm for stealing and gains control of their company and what will become the Goblin Formula.

GOOD DAY

When Osborn shoots the Skrull Queen Veranke live on TV, he is hailed a hero for ending the Skrulls' Secret Invasion of Earth. The U.S. president even makes the cunning villain head of S.H.I.E.L.D.!

WHEN BAD GUYS GET WORSE!

Osborn becomes U.S.A. security chief and renames S.H.I.E.L.D. H.A.M.M.E.R. He also dons one of Tony Stark's Iron Man suits and names himself the Iron Patriot, leading a new team of Dark Avengers. Osborn hopes to present himself to the world as a combination of Iron Man and Captain America, but his evil side soon resurfaces!

GOBLIN GOONS

The Goblin Nation are followers of the Green Goblin, wearing Goblin-themed garb and using Osborn's Goblin technology.

TOP 5
Goblin Formula Effects

1. **SUPERHUMAN STRENGTH** – as well as enhanced speed, reflexes and endurance!

2. **REGENERATION** – heals quickly: Osborn has even grown back lost limbs and organs!

3. **SUPERIOR INTELLIGENCE** – Osborn was already clever, but the formula makes him a genius!

4. **INSANITY** – Osborn must wear drug patches on his skin to keep sane, though they don't always seem to work very well!

5. **ALTERED APPEARANCE** – Norman may look the same in this universe (he wears a mask when Green Goblin), but other people are not so lucky!

INSANE AND LOVING IT!

Norman Osborn is the unbelievably wealthy chief of tech company **OsCorp**. He's been **head of U.S.A. security**, but he's really motivated by **greed** and an unquenchable **thirst for power**. Oh, and he **really hates** Spider-Man, too!

$1 million

Daily Bugle's bounty for Spider-Man's capture on behalf of Norman Osborn.

FAST FACTS

FULL NAME: Norman Virgil Osborn

ALIASES: Green Goblin, Iron Patriot, Goblin King

STRENGTHS: Ruthless businessman, cunning strategist, skilled in chemistry, electronics, engineering, and genetics.

WEAKNESSES: Goblin Formula has alarming side effects that undermine his schemes

ALLIES: Makes brief alliances with other villains, but he's only looking out for himself!

ENEMIES: Spider-Man, Iron Man, Captain America, Avengers

"Now... just between me and you, here's my little **SECRET**. Here's what it all **MEANS**...

S.H.I.E.L.D. DECLASSIFIED

OSBORN'S DOWNFALL
U.S. security chief, Osborn organises an illegal attack on Asgard, which is floating in the sky above Broxton, Oklahoma. Not one but two Captain Americas – and many other heroes – try to foil his plan, but Asgard is destroyed. By now, it is clear to everyone that Osborn is crazy with power and he is sacked in disgrace.

BEST KNOWN FOR **POWER-MAD SCHEMES AND PLOTTING SPIDEY'S DOOM**

FAMILY CONNECTIONS
One complicated, messed-up family!

NORMAN OSBORN
Criminally insane patriarch

HAROLD "HARRY" OSBORN
Son of Norman and wife Emily, who dies after Harry is born. Troubled Harry follows in Norman's freaky footsteps as Green Goblin and joins his Avengers team as American Son.

GWEN STACY
Mother of Goblin-Formula-infected twins Gabriel and Sarah after secret affair with Norman. Gwen wants Norman to keep away from her kids. Killed by Norman as Green Goblin, who blames Peter Parker.

GABRIEL STACY
Joins Norman's Dark Avengers team as the second American Son. Goblin Formula eventually drives him insane.

SARAH STACY
Daughter Sarah tries to use her abilities for good!

...The bad guys **ALWAYS** win."

YECCH!

After losing control of H.A.M.M.E.R. and suffering repeated defeats, Norman becomes the Goblin King. His "realm" becomes the New York City sewer system!

"Venom wants to PLAY!"

AAARRGHH!!! The Venom symbiote busts Eddie Brock out of jail and leaves behind **AN OFFSPRING.** This bonds with Brock's cellmate, violent **CLETUS KASADAY,** who becomes the **RAMPAGING VILLAIN CARNAGE.**

Q: What is a Symbiote?

A: It's one of a species of **alien parasites** called the **Klyntar.** A symbiote **sets out to be good,** but if it bonds with a less-than-perfect host, it becomes **vicious and violent.**

BEST KNOWN FOR

POSSESSING SPIDER-MAN'S POWERS – ALONG WITH SHARP TEETH AND A TERRIBLE TONGUE

WHEN GOOD GUYS

Eddie Brock is a respected journalist until he pens an exposé blaming an innocent man for a crime that is later solved by Spider-Man. Brock blames Spidey for his downfall, making him an ideal host for the sneaky Venom symbiote!

Q: How does Spidey get rid of the symbiote?

A: With the help of **Reed Richards,** Spider-Man discovers that the symbiote can't stand loud noises, such as **the clanging of church bells.**

ALTERNATE UNIVERSE

A **pig version** of Venom named **Pork Grind** faces off against Peter Porker, the **Spectacular Spider-Ham!**

VENOM
The Venom symbiote bonds with Eddie Brock to create one of Spider-Man's most deadly foes.

CARNAGE
Criminal Cletus Kasaday is the symbiote's host in this crazy and very deadly partnership.

TOXIN
Ex-cop Pat Mulligan succeeds Eddie Brock as Toxin and becomes an ally of the Avengers.

ANTI-VENOM
This mindless creature forms from the remnants of the Venom symbiote in Eddie Brock's blood.

Power Up!

CHANGEUP
Exposed to crime Mister Negative's inverting touch, Eddie Brock's skin transforms part of the Venom symbiote into Anti-Venom, capable of "curing" Spider-Man of his powers – and much more, too!

S.H.I.E.L.D. DECLASSIFIED

AGENT VENOM
War hero Corporal Eugene "Flash" Thompson loses his legs fighting in Iraq and the government selects him to be Agent Venom – a super agent harnessing the power of a subdued Venom symbiote. He is outfitted with a "kill switch" in case he loses control!

BAD DAY

Trapped on **an alien Battleworld** in a tattered costume, Spider-Man dons what he believes to be a suit of **alien fabric,** but he soon discovers that **the suit is alive!**

HOMESICK SUIT
Flash Thompson's control over his symbiote suit becomes increasingly erratic after he joins the Guardians of the Galaxy. The symbiote even hijacks the Guardians' ship and takes it to its home planet!

VENOMISED!

Spider-Man thinks his **cool black suit** is just an **alien costume** – until it begins to **control him!** He gets rid of this **symbiote,** but it moves on, creating the **villain Venom** – and **even worse foes.**

COST-EFFECTIVE
One of the **major perks** of the Venom symbiote? A **self-replenishing supply** of webbing. No risk of **running out mid-swing** between two skyscrapers.

When Doc Ock's eyesight fails, he wires his prosthetic vision goggles directly into his brain. However, the loose-fitting goggles fall out of his head!

MECHANICAL MENACE
Doctor Octopus has doctorates in nuclear physics and biochemistry. He invents his harness with mechanical arms to conduct dangerous experiments from a safe distance. A lab accident bombards him with radiation, and the harness fuses to his body.

ARMS CRISIS!

Otto Octavius was the genius son of a brutal construction worker. He becomes a top scientist, but his **power-mad ambitions** lead him to become the villainous **Doctor Octopus** and a **bitter foe** of **Spider-Man!**

HANDLE WITH CARE!

Otto's four mechanical **titanium** tentacles can each perform a different task simultaneously.

AAAARRGHH!!!

KAINE, a crazy clone of Peter Parker, appears out of nowhere and **BUMPS OFF** Doc Ock! The poor doctor had just **SAVED** Peter's life!

NUMBER CRUNCH!

360°
Spinning rotation of each tentacle's pincers

111kg (245lbs)
Otto's weight

80kph (50mph)
Speed when walking on tentacles

13cm (5in)
Diameter of Otto's tentacles

1.8–7.6m (6–25ft)
Distance Otto's arms extend

98kph (61mph)
Speed Otto's tentacles can strike

WHAT?!

Prison doctors remove Doc Ock's tentacles. Little do they know... he can **mentally control** his arms! He gets them back – simply by sending the **thought impulse**: "Return to your master!"

WHEN BAD GUYS GO GOOD!

SUPERIOR SPIDEY!
Doc Ock's health is failing. Before he dies, he swaps minds with Peter Parker, so Peter dies in Doc Ock's body and Ock takes over Spider-Man's body. Doc Ock becomes the "Superior Spider-Man", aiming to be a better hero than Peter Parker ever was!

WOW!

1,448

The distance in km (900 miles) Otto can telepathically control his tentacles.

FAST FACTS

REAL NAME:
Dr Otto Octavius

ALIASES: Doctor Octopus, Doc Ock, Master Planner

ALLIES: Sinister Six, Masters of Evil, Charlotte Witter

ENEMIES: Spider-Man

STRENGTHS: Intellect (gifted in science and engineering), four mechanical tentacles

WEAKNESSES: Poor eyesight, failing health

REALLY?!

Doc Ock rents a room from Peter Parker's Aunt May. When he learns she's set to inherit a nuclear reactor, Otto tries to **marry her!**

GOOD DAY

Sometimes Doc Ock **really scores!** During their first encounter at Bliss Private Hospital, Doc Ock beats Spider-Man so badly that Spidey **wants to retire!** When the Fantastic Four decline to fight him, Doc Ock appears to have **won...**

UPGRADED!

Doc Ock upgrades from four to eight tentacles and then tries to control all the electronics in New York City!

TELL ME MORE!

Doc Ock doesn't always battle Spidey alone... he forms the Sinister Six – himself plus Vulture, Electro, Kraven, Lizard and Mysterio – to try to destroy the web-slinger!

"With such power and my brilliant mind, I'm the **SUPREME** being on Earth!"

BEFORE...

"Mad scientist" Doc Ock has a suitably loopy fashion sense that changes with the times without ever achieving cool!

Otto begins his villainous career in a green jumpsuit and unflattering "bowl" haircut.

He then attempts classy, with a white suit and sunglasses. Still the same bad haircut!

More recently, Otto has sported a flowing trench coat and weird slicked-back hair.

AFTER...

REALLY?!

When the **renegade heroes of Nextwave** visit the town of Shotcreek, they discover that it's being attacked by **Rorkannu** and **his army of Mindless Ones**. Rorkannu could be Dormammu's **long-lost twin brother...**

Umar Loves Hulk!

Umar likes her men tall, green and angry! When Hulk is close to destroying Earth, she takes him to the Dark Dimension as her new husband. She gets a "handsome" new king, and the Hulk has fun smashing Mindless Ones!

BACK FROM THE DEAD!

Dormammu and his sister Umar have a **love-hate** relationship! Dormammu kills Umar — but she is brought back by the power of **a wishing well!**

Q: Who are the Mindless Ones?

A: These **one-eyed brutes** inhabit the fringes of the **Dark Dimension** and destroy everything they can with their stony fists and eye-beams. Dormammu sets up **magical barriers** to stop them from **destroying** the entire **Dark Dimension!**

FAMILY CONNECTIONS

Clea — Doctor Strange

Umar

Dormammu's **sister, Umar,** is sometimes his ally and sometimes his rival! Umar has a **daughter** named **Clea.** Unlike her mother and uncle, Clea rejects evil. She falls for **hunky Doctor Strange** when he visits Dormammu's Dark Dimension!

AAAARRGHH!!

Doctor Strange stops **THE MINDLESS ONES** from invading Dormammu's domain and makes him promise to leave Earth alone. Dormammu **SWEARS REVENGE!**

DOUBLE TROUBLE

DORMAMMU & LOKI

This devious duo cook up a plan to get the Avengers and Defenders fighting over the mystic **Evil Eye of Avalon.** When Loki betrays Dormammu, the Dread One **ensnares him** with magic – but then the Scarlet Witch **traps Dormammu** in the Evil Eye!

FAST FACTS

REAL NAME: Dormammu

ALIASES: The Dread One, Lord of the Dark Dimension

SPECIES: Faltine (magical entities from another reality)

STRENGTHS: Total mastery of magic; can draw on the power of his worshippers and the magical energies of the Dark Dimension itself!

WEAKNESS: Ruling one dimension just isn't enough!

FOES: Doctor Strange, the Ancient One, Clea, Celestials, Eternity

"No mere mortal can overcome DORMAMMU!"

TOP 5
Dormammu Defeats

1 **DORMAMMU** – challenges Doctor Strange to a fight in front of the other Lords of the Netherworld, but is outwitted by the Sorcerer Supreme.

2 **DORMAMMU** – attacks the mighty cosmic being Eternity and, after a battle that nearly destroys the universe, is crushed between two planets!!

3 **DOCTOR STRANGE** – tricks Dormammu into going through a portal to Earth, thus breaking his mystic oath to leave the Earth alone! Violating this oath drains his power!

4 **DORMAMMU** – traps the Earth spirit Gaea and tries to conquer Earth, but Umar helps Doctor Strange banish him from our world!

5 **DOCTOR STRANGE AND CLEA** – lead a rebellion against Dormammu and Clea takes his Dark Dimension throne!

BETWEEN...
Marvel's Stan Lee made up the name Dormammu as something cool for Dr Strange to say when spell-casting. Fans wanted to know more, and the Dread One debuted in *Strange Tales* #126 (November 1964).
...THE PANELS

TELL ME MORE!
Plokta, a demonic Dark Dimension entity, creates the Mindless Ones from the souls of people trapped in an apartment block in Birmingham, U.K.!

Power Up!
ABSORBING THE ENEMY
When **UMAR AND BARON MORDO** take over the Dark Dimension, a mysterious Faltine helps **CLEA** fight them. It is actually **DORMAMMU** in disguise! He absorbs Mordo and Umar and becomes **EVEN MORE POWERFUL!**

DREAD LORD
This flame-headed, **mystical ruler** of the hellish **Dark Dimension** is pure evil. **Dormammu** is obsessed with **conquering Earth** and destroying its Sorcerer Supreme, **Doctor Strange!**

BARONS OF BAD

FULL NAME:
Baron Heinrich Zemo

BIRTHPLACE: Castle Zemo, Germany

STRENGTHS: Scientific genius, slowed aging, expert marksman and swordfighter

WEAKNESSES: Obsessive hatred for Captain America, crazy for power

ALLIES: Masters of Evil, Baron von Strucker, Red Skull

FOES: Captain America, Nick Fury and his Howling Commandos, Fantastic Four, Invader

Q: What's with the mask?

A: During **World War II**, Heinrich Zemo is Hitler's greatest **scientist**. After Heinrich's **death ray** kills hundreds of Germans, he becomes such a **hated figure** in his own country that he starts wearing a **purple hood** to conceal his identity!

Q: Why does Zemo age so slowly?

A: **Compound X!** Heinrich invents this serum to preserve his **youth** and keep him in **prime** physical condition. His son Helmut **bathes** in it!

BARON
HEINRICH ZEMO

GOOD DAY

Heinrich **captures Cap** and ties him to a **plane** which explodes over the **Arctic**. Heinrich believes he has **finally killed** his archenemy! But Cap survives, after being **frozen in ice** for decades...

AAAARRGHH!!!
Heinrich is **DAZZLED** by light reflecting off Captain America's shield and misfires his weapon – bringing a **DEADLY LANDSLIDE** of **ROCKS** crashing down on himself!

"I warn you... it is DANGEROUS to pry into Zemo's secrets!"

HANDLE WITH CARE!

Heinrich develops an indestructible **glue, Adhesive X**, to immobilise Allied troops. When Captain America breaks a vat of Adhesive X with his shield, the glue **spills** all over Heinrich's head and **sticks** his hood **permanently** to his face!

There is more than one **Baron Zemo** and **both** are bitter foes of **Captain America!** Baron **Heinrich** Zemo is an **evil genius** and **war criminal,** and his son, **Helmut,** is a **lawless opportunist** on a mission to **avenge his father!**

Family business!
After Baron Heinrich comes to a sticky end, Helmut **inherits his title.** Later on, the new Baron also carries on the **legacy** of the Super Villain team his dad created, the **Masters of Evil.** Helmut starts up **two new teams,** hoping to punish the Avengers for his **father's demise!**

FAST FACTS

FULL NAME:
Baron Helmut Zemo

BIRTHPLACE: Leipzig, Germany

STRENGTHS: Slowed aging, expert combatant, more cunning than his dad

WEAKNESSES: Overconfidence – taking over the world is never easy!

ALLIES: Songbird, Moonstone, Atlas, Masters of Evil, Thunderbolts, Hydra

FOES: Captain America, Bucky Barnes, Norman Osborn, Doctor Doom, Avengers

FAMILY CONNECTIONS
Helmut's wife, Hieke, is a villain known as the **Baroness.** She once claimed to be a **reincarnation** of Heinrich Zemo in a **woman's body...** and it may even be the truth! The happy couple adopt **25 children,** the **Kinder,** whom they **brainwash** to **hate** Captain America!

YECCH!
Helmut tries to boil Cap in a vat of Adhesive X. The Baron's face gets splashed with glue and ends up **horribly scarred,** looking like **drippy melted wax!**

HANDLE WITH CARE!
Helmut gets hold of **twin gems** named "moonstones", which are actually **Kree lifestones.** They allow him to travel across **space and time,** and **between dimensions.** When the stones get cracked, however, they hurl Helmut through a **time vortex!**

BAD DAY
Helmut and his **Masters of Evil** team are the first to destroy the **Avengers' Mansion.** But his triumph is shortlived – Helmut is defeated in battle and appears to **fall to his death** from the roof...

BARON HELMUT ZEMO

*"**GUIDE** my hand, my father—as I avenge your **DEATH!**"*

The underworld will now be run like a *BUSINESS*... and the *CHAIRMAN OF THE BOARD* will be ... *THE KINGPIN!*

TELL ME MORE!

Kingpin Wilson Fisk may look fat and out of shape, but he is actually 191kg (420lbs) of solid muscle! Fisk is also a martial arts master – he regularly beats up a gang of burly bruisers as part of his fitness program. Mess with him at your peril!

HANDLE WITH CARE!

The Kingpin's **jewelled walking stick** contains a nasty surprise – its inbuilt **disintegrator ray** can **vaporize** an opponent!

TOP 5

Kingpin's Flawed Henchmen

1 ELEKTRA
PROS: a highly trained ninja assassin
CONS: has a thing for Kingpin's nemesis, Daredevil

2 BULLSEYE
PROS: an incredibly accurate assassin
CONS: better at killing than following orders

3 NUKE
PROS: a Captain America-style super-soldier
CONS: goes out of control and devastates Manhattan

4 TYPHOID MARY
PROS: a mutant with amazing psychic powers
CONS: dangerously crazy and seriously unpredictable

5 SANDMAN
PROS: his ability to turn to sand is a powerful weapon
CONS: keeps getting outsmarted by Spider-Man

NOOOOO!! **PETER PARKER** reveals that he is actually **SPIDER-MAN** and **THE KINGPIN** sends a sniper to shoot him. The bullet hits **AUNT MAY** instead!

TOP CRIME BOSSES

KINGPIN

A hugely powerful, ambitious and ruthless criminal genius

THE ROSE

Kingpin's son Richard Fisk tries to take over dad's operation

HAMMERHEAD

Violent, retro-styled mobster with a steel-plated head

SILVIO "SILVERMANE" MANFREDI

Aging Maggia boss who turns himself into a cyborg to cheat death

COUNT NEFARIA

Gains the powers of Whirlwind, Living Laser and Power Man

MADAME MASQUE

The daughter of Count Nefaria, her gold mask hides a scarred face

TOMBSTONE

Lonnie Lincoln files his teeth to points, making him even more scary

JUSTIN HAMMER

Criminal genius specialising in financial wheeling and dealing

THE HOOD

Parker Robins gains superpowers from the demon Dormammu

MR. NEGATIVE

Controls the Darkforce to shape-shift and also brainwash people

HEADBANGER!
The **gangster** Hammerhead **takes out** enemies with his reinforced **steel skull!**

Q: Who are the Maggia?

A: **The Maggia** originated in southern Europe and is now a **major power** in the U.S. underworld. Members promise to **keep silent** about group activities, on **pain of death.** There are three rival Maggia "families", each led by a notorious mobster: the **Silvermane** family, the **Nefaria** family and the **Hammerhead** family.

WHO'S THE BOSS?

These **crime lords** are cunning, ruthless and command gangs of henchmen, making them **dangerous foes.** Some even find ways to **boost their power,** becoming Super Villains able to battle the champions of justice **one-on-one!**

MAGICAL MENACES

From **demons** and **godlike beings** to **evil magicians,** the universe is **constantly under threat** from sorcerous villains. All that stands between Earth and **certain destruction** is a handful of courageous **mystic heroes,** armed with a library of **awesome spells!**

REALLY?!

Sorceress **Morgan le Fay** first meets **Doctor Doom** and **Iron Man** in the time of **King Arthur** – and mistakes the time-travelling duo for **armoured knights!** The evil Morgan and "Lord Doom" **join forces,** but are defeated by **"Sir Iron Man"!**

BETWEEN...

The demon Thog the Nether-Spawn was once defeated by Marvel Comics writer Steve Gerber! Steve wrote *Man-Thing* #22 (October 1975), in which he and Man-Thing save the universe from Thog!

...THE PANELS

BAD DAY

Magician Baron Mordo is a student of the wise Ancient One, but, **hungry for power,** he plots to **kill his master.** Doctor Strange **saves the day** – and becomes Mordo's mortal enemy!

Power Up!

BLACK MAGIC
Villains Baron Mordo and Dormammu both **HATE** Doctor Strange, so they make a deal: Dormammu gives Mordo unlimited magical power – so he can **DESTROY** the Sorcerer Supreme!

AAAARRGHH!!

The sorcerer **BELASCO** plans to sacrifice **SHANNA THE SHE-DEVIL** to bring the evil **ELDER GODS** back to Earth. Shanna's boyfriend **KA-ZAR** saves her – so the Elder Gods imprison him in Limbo!

Power Up!

DEMON HULKBUSTER!
Doctor Strange tries to use the demon **ZOM** to stop a rampaging Hulk, but **SETS ZOM FREE!** Zom takes over the Hulkbuster armour and seems unbeatable – until his spirit is captured by Strange's loyal assistant, **WONG!**

AAARRGHH!! CHONDU THE MYSTIC has had a lot of bodies! His mind is put into the hero **NIGHTHAWK**, then into a **FAWN**, before he ends up in a **TENTACLE-ARMED MONSTER BODY!**

TOP 5
MERLIN WANNABES
Several magicians have claimed to be the legendary Merlin!

Enchantress

HOW ENCHANTING!
Asgardian sorceress Enchantress uses her power and beauty to get her way. She often tricks the Executioner into helping her, but her main target is Thor, whom she thinks should rule Asgard – with her by his side!

MERLYN – an Omniversal Guardian and advisor to Captain Britain.

MAD MERLIN – a villain who battled Thor while pretending to be Merlin, and later fought the X-Men as "Warlock" and "Maha Yogi".

COSMIC MERLIN – a mysterious figure who once helped Captain Britain.

ALIEN MERLIN – fought the Avengers, and turned out to be an evil shape-shifting Dire Wraith!

DOUBLE TROUBLE

CALYPSO & KRAVEN
Voodoo priestess Calypso is obsessed with helping Kraven the Hunter kill Spider-Man. She uses a magical drum and mind-bending poisons to weaken Spidey, but Kraven lets him go when he realises Calypso is using magic – Kraven likes a fair fight!

TEAM PLAYER
Enchantress disguises herself as the hero **Valkyrie** and recruits a woman-only team of Avengers. Naming themselves the **Lady Liberators**, they take on the Avengers to prove they are **just as strong** as Earth's Mightiest Heroes!

ALBION – this member of the Knights of Pendragon may actually be a reincarnation of the legendary wizard!

MONSTERS: Carrion (Malcolm McBride), Lizard (Dr Curtis Connors)

MATTER MANIPULATORS: Graviton (Franklin Hall)

ENERGY BEINGS: Klaw (Ulysses Klaw), Living Laser (Arthur Parks)

SUPER SCIENTISTS: Grey Gargoyle (Paul Duval), Molten Man (Mark Raxton)

HANDLE WITH CARE!

Klaw **assassinates** Black Panther (T'Chaka), but **loses** to his sucessor, T'Challa. To become stronger, he swaps his hand for a **sonic blaster** and jumps into a sonic conversion device, becoming a being of **living sound.**

NUMBER CRUNCH!

261kg (575lbs)
Weight gained by Paul Duval when he becomes Grey Gargoyle

249kg (550lbs)
Lizard and Molten Man's weight

260°C (500°F)
Maximum temperature Molten Man can withstand

113kph (70mph)
Lizard's tail whip speed

40 tons
Heaviest weight Molten Man can lift

Power Up!

FUN WITH LASERS!
Tony Stark believes **ARTHUR PARKS** has been killed in an explosion. In fact, Tony's Iron Man suit has accidentally **CAPTURED** Arthur's scattered particles. Arthur then re-forms as the **LIVING LASER!**

TOP 6
SCIENTIFIC SUPERPOWERS

GREY GARGOYLE – turns victims to stone for one hour with a touch of his right hand.

THE LIZARD – regrows severed limbs and telepathically controls other reptiles.

MOLTEN MAN – emits heat and harmful radiation.

GRAVITON – power over gravity; he can fly, and crush opponents into the ground!

KLAW – made of living sound; creates other objects made of pure audio.

LIVING LASER – made entirely of photons; uses his own body as a weapon.

STONE COLD VILLAINY

Chemist **Paul Duval** spills a potion on his hand, turning it to **living stone**. He gains the ability to **transform his entire body** into living stone, and turn others into **statues** with a **single touch!** In stone form, Duval gains vast **strength** and **durability** as the indestructible criminal **Grey Gargoyle!**

ARMED AND DANGEROUS!
After Dr Curtis Connors loses his arm in the military, he becomes obsessed with reptiles that can regrow limbs and develops a serum using their DNA. The serum regrows his arm, but turns him into the giant Lizard!

AFTER...

YEGGH!

The original "living corpse" known as Carrion (a clone of Jackal, Miles Warren) creates a tentacled Spider-Amoeba using Peter Parker's DNA. Spider-Man throws the monster at Carrion – and it eats him!

BAD SCIENCE

Viruses, chemicals, serums, radiation, toxic pollutants, alien alloys... By **scientific slipup** or **risky experiment**, these **dangerous substances** can turn normal people into **misfits, monsters and super-powered villains!**

WHEN GOOD GUYS GO BAD!

IF YOU CAN'T BEAT 'EM – JOIN 'EM!
At first, kindly Dr Curtis Connors tries to resist the Lizard inside. Eventually, he uses the Lizard as an excuse to do evil. He even transforms his son into a lizard sidekick!

WOW!

299,792

The speed Living Laser can travel in km per second (186,282 miles per second).

 TELL ME MORE!

Scientist Mark Raxton develops a liquid metallic alloy from a radioactive meteor, but spills it on himself and transforms into the villainous Molten Man. His step-sister, Liz (Harry Osborn's wife), helps him reform, but he doesn't lose his fiery temper!

1 **M.O.D.O.K.** – creates Red Hulk and Red She-Hulk.

2 **TINKERER** – creates the whip-like, spiked, poisonous tail of the villain Scorpion.

3 **PROF. SPENCER SMYTHE** – invents various Spider-Slayer robots to attack Spider-Man.

4 **JACKAL** – creates clones to challenge, confuse and menace Spidey!

5 **DR. KARL MALUS** – invents a control collar to make Werewolf By Night attack Spider-Woman.

6 **MAD THINKER** – his Awesome Android mimics the physical properties of anything it touches.

7 **EGGHEAD** – invents a machine to turn ants against Ant-Man!

8 **WIZARD** – his antigravity discs send three of the Fantastic Four floating away like balloons.

9 **MORBIUS** – creates an experimental serum that accidentally turns him into a "living vampire".

10 **CALVIN ZABO** – his "Hyde formula" enhances strength, but induces violent rages.

WOW!

340

Evil humanoid supercomputer M.O.D.O.K.'s weight in kg (750lbs).

BEST KNOWN FOR

BEING TOO CLEVER FOR THEIR OWN GOOD – AND EVERYONE ELSE'S!

Nooooo!!

WIZARD captures Carnage and tries to turn him into his own **EVIL AGENT**. He transfers the symbiote into the body of **DR KARL MALUS**, but the plan soon goes **HORRIBLY WRONG!**

UPGRADED!

When Spencer Smythe's son, Alastair, ends up in a wheelchair, he builds a hideous biomechanical exoskeleton to not only walk, but also destroy Spider-Man – becoming the Ultimate Spider-Slayer!

IDENTITY CRISIS!

The Jackal creates a virus that gives everyone in Manhattan spider powers, robbing Spider-Man of his advantage – and his unique identity!

AARRGHH!

J. Jonah Jameson pays Prof Spencer Smythe to create a ROBOT with spider-powers so that Jameson can capture SPIDEY himself!

FAST FACTS

EVIL AND LOVING IT: M.O.D.O.K, Jackal, Dr Faustus, Mister Hyde, Leader, Mad Thinker, Wizard

SCIENTISTS DOING BAD THINGS: Tinkerer, Prof Spencer Smythe, Egghead, Red Ghost, Dr Karl Malus

MAKING AMENDS: Morbius, Maximus

HANDLE WITH CARE!

The **Tinkerer** is the most sought-after inventor in the **criminal underworld!** His clients include Hobgoblin, Beetle, Mysterio, Big Wheel and the Constrictor. He also develops Trapster's arsenal, Grim Reaper's **scythe** and Diamondback's **throwing diamonds!**

DASTARDLY DEED

Smooth-talking psychiatrist Dr Faustus tries to drive Captain America nuts. Cap thinks he's back fighting in the dark days of World War II – until Faustus's mind-bending drugs wear off!

LAB RATS!

Every villainous **organisation** bent on **world domination** or destruction needs its own evil **genius** to design **doomsday devices,** build superweapons or **enslave minds!** And sometimes these masterminds go into business for themselves!

BEFORE...

Scientist Calvin Zabo develops a formula to transform himself into Mister Hyde. He gains 91kg (200lbs) of muscle and bone in just 30 seconds and turns into a grotesque, muscular fiend!

Calvin Zabo – a clever, physically unremarkable medical research scientist.

Mister Hyde – a villain so formidable that Baron Zemo recruits him for his Masters of Evil.

AFTER...

Q: Who are M.O.D.O.K's 11?

A: When M.O.D.O.K. plans to steal a living star and sell it to A.I.M. (then Hydra's scientific wing) for a cool $1 billion, he gathers a team of villains to help: Mandarin, Chameleon (Ultra-Adaptoid in disguise), Spot, Living Laser, Puma, Mentallo, Monica Rappaccini, Armadillo, Rocket Racer and Nightshade.

BIG-HEADED!

Being exposed to gamma rays covers labourer Samuel Sterns with boils, swells his head, turns him green and makes him a science genius! As the Leader, he dreams of controlling the Hulk and conquering the world.

IF LOOKS COULD KILL

You **can't always spot** a Super Villain from his or her **appearance,** but these rogues' rough-around-the-edges features are a dead giveaway. They all possess **looks** that could **kill** – sometimes literally!

FAST FACTS

VILLAINOUS VISAGES:
M.O.D.O.K., Gorgolla, 8-Ball, Xemnu, Terror, Karkas, Arnim Zola, the Headmen, Mojo

LETHAL LOOKERS:
Basilisk, the Orb, Skein, the Needle, Doctor Bong

TOP 3

Calling Cards of Pool-Themed Criminal, 8-Ball

1 **INVENTS** a hovercraft shaped like a pool rack.

2 **FIGHTS DO-GOODERS** with a jet-propelled cue-stick and ball bombs.

3 **NAMES** his henchmen after other pool balls!

SPECIAL MOVES
When **Doctor Bong** strikes his **bell-shaped helmet** with his metal ball hand, he can create **powerful vibrations, stun foes** or even trigger his **teleportation device.**

AAAARRGHH!!
Eight-legged **MOJO** is not just really **UGLY** – on Earth, his whole body acts as an **ANTI-LIFE FORCE** that causes everything to **SHRIVEL UP** and **DIE!**

SPECIAL MOVES

The immortal **Terror** was an ordinary human, until he slew a demon and was cursed to take on its **spiky skin** and **decaying form**. When he **loses a body part,** he exudes an **acid** that loosens a body part from another person and **sticks it** to his **own** body!

YECCH!

One of evil scientist **M.O.D.O.K.'s** many doomsday plans revolves around a **living supercomputer** built from his own **cloned brains!**

6

The number of long spikes on Terror's face. He breaks them off to use as weapons and then regrows them!

WHAT?!

She-Hulk defeats the **furry criminal alien Xemnu** by convincing a much bigger alien that Xemnu is a **teddy bear** for it to play with!

TEAM PLAYER

Elderly tailor **Josef Saint** loses an eye in a mugging, but discovers he can **paralyse people** with his remaining one! He renames himself the **Needle** and joins the **Night Shift** villain group.

Power Up!

THE EYES HAVE IT

Basilisk's **GLEAMING RED EYES** project energy beams that can **FLASH-FREEZE** or **SUPERHEAT** his foes and also **LEVITATE** Basilisk and move him through the air!

MONSTER MASH

It's behind you! From **killer crabs** and **city-sacking beasts** to a **creepy monster** that appears out of a **painting** – many of these creatures are the **stuff of nightmares.** That's **bad news** for even the **toughest** of Super Heroes!

REALLY?!

A pilot crashes on **Easter Island** in the Pacific and learns a terrible secret! The **giant statues** for which the isle is famous are actually **rocky-skinned aliens** called **Lithodia Rexians,** and they are planning to **take over Earth.** Even worse, when the pilot tries to warn people, they think he's **crazy!**

Titano

Gomdulla

S.H.I.E.L.D. DECLASSIFIED

ISLAND ISOLATION
Weird beasties of all kinds roam free on Monster Isle, off the coast of Japan. The Fantastic Four in particular use this jumbo-sized wildlife reserve to keep creatures they've captured from doing any more damage!

18,000,000,000

The weight of the Apocalypse Beast in tons.
This 4.8-kilometre-high (3 miles) multi-eyed alien is the terror of Tokyo!

6 MONSTER-DEFEATING TECHNIQUES

1 FLYSWATTER – shape-shifter alien Zogg turns into a housefly and gets squished!

2 TERMITES – a swarm nibbles the wooden alien Groot to kindling!

3 OFF SWITCH – Gomdulla can be deactivated by pressing a button on his right foot!

4 GLACIER – Titano is stuck solid when he gets trapped in Arctic ice!

5 ANTS – Grottu, King of the Insects, is foiled when his own "followers" turn against him.

6 QUICKSAND – Troublesome Googam is helpless when he gets stuck in mud!

DASTARDLY DEED!

Human-mutants known as the **Deviants** are obsessed with creating **ever-more-horrible monsters**. The Deviant **priest-scientists** enjoy making bizarre mutants to use as **living weapons**!

TOP 5
Awesome Creatures

1 FIN FANG FOOM, HE WHOSE LIMBS SHATTER MOUNTAINS AND WHOSE BACK SCRAPES THE SUN – a fire-breathing alien dragon-beast.

2 IT, THE LIVING COLOSSUS – a statue that comes to life and smashes up Moscow and Los Angeles!

3 GOMDULLA THE LIVING PHARAOH – a massive mummy with a very bad attitude!

4 ZZUTAK, THE THING THAT SHOULDN'T EXIST – a monster that emerges from a painting created with magic pigments!

5 TITANO, THE MONSTER THAT TIME FORGOT – a giant crab from the ocean depths!

THEY AREN'T ALL BAD!
The alien **Googam**, the robotic **Electro**, the primate **Gorgilla** and the dragon **Fin Fang Foom** are freed from captivity and **give up** their **villainous ways**. When they aren't busy at their day jobs, they fight menaces like the **extra dimensional warlord Tim Boo Ba** as the heroic **Fin Fang Four**!

"That's right, Earthlings... cower before the all-powerful Goom!"

GOOGAM

FAMILY CONNECTIONS
When **big-toothed** alien **Goom** is **arrested** for trying to conquer Earth, he leaves his son **Googam** behind in a cave. Googam soon emerges and tries to **take over the world**, but he proves **just as hopeless** as his dad!

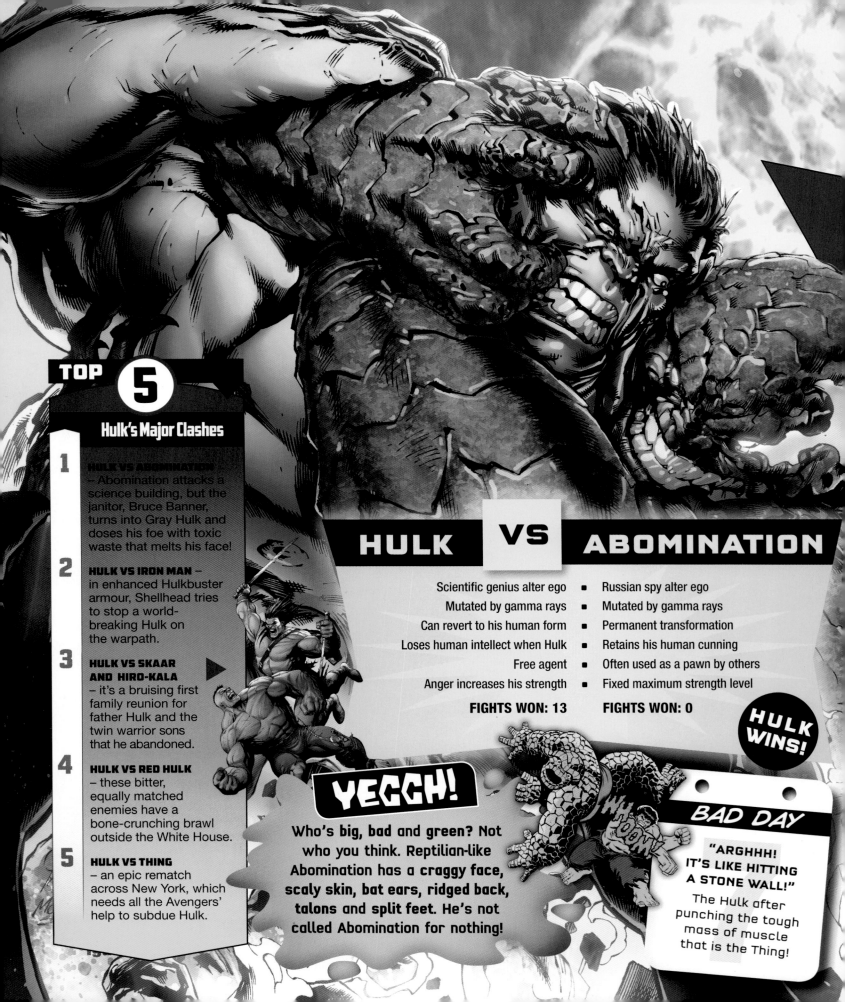

TOP **5**

Hulk's Major Clashes

1 **HULK VS ABOMINATION** – Abomination attacks a science building, but the janitor, Bruce Banner, turns into Gray Hulk and doses his foe with toxic waste that melts his face!

2 **HULK VS IRON MAN** – in enhanced Hulkbuster armour, Shellhead tries to stop a world-breaking Hulk on the warpath.

3 **HULK VS SKAAR AND HIRO-KALA** – it's a bruising first family reunion for father Hulk and the twin warrior sons that he abandoned.

4 **HULK VS RED HULK** – these bitter, equally matched enemies have a bone-crunching brawl outside the White House.

5 **HULK VS THING** – an epic rematch across New York, which needs all the Avengers' help to subdue Hulk.

HULK **VS** ABOMINATION

Scientific genius alter ego	■ Russian spy alter ego
Mutated by gamma rays	■ Mutated by gamma rays
Can revert to his human form	■ Permanent transformation
Loses human intellect when Hulk	■ Retains his human cunning
Free agent	■ Often used as a pawn by others
Anger increases his strength	■ Fixed maximum strength level

FIGHTS WON: 13   **FIGHTS WON: 0**

HULK WINS!

YECCH!

Who's big, bad and green? Not who you think. Reptilian-like Abomination has a craggy face, scaly skin, bat ears, ridged back, talons and split feet. He's not called Abomination for nothing!

BAD DAY

"ARGHHH! IT'S LIKE HITTING A STONE WALL!" The Hulk after punching the tough mass of muscle that is the Thing!

Power Up!

KLUH DESTROY!
Kluh is a Hulk incarnation who emerges when the Hulk is overwhelmed by **SADNESS**. This monstrous menace **TRASHES** the Avengers and only wants to wreak **DEATH** and **DESTRUCTION!**

YECCH!

In a battle between the Ultimate Hulk and Wolverine, the Green Giant pulls his opponent in two – and **throws** the top half miles away. Wolvie will have to spend **months** crawling back to his **legs!**

Ouch!
How do you defeat a furious Hulk? **Crawl into his ear!** One of the Avengers' **smallest** members, the Wasp, climbs in and **zaps** his skull repeatedly with her **sting** power!

TEMPER, TEMPER!

The rampaging Hulk has fought **almost everyone –** from **malevolent monsters** and **earthbound enemies** to **cosmic crusaders.** Yet no matter what they throw at him, the result is the same... you **can't keep Hulk down!**

TOP 4
HULK VS RHINO BATTLES
Some of the Hulk's wackiest battles have been with this horn-headed henchman!

NOoooo!!
Hulk declares war on the Illuminati – and he seems unstoppable in his **WORLD-BREAKER** form! It only ends when Hulk **BEGS** Iron Man to use an **ORBITAL LASER** on him – before he destroys the planet!

WHEN GOOD GUYS GO BAD!

WELCOME TO THE TEAM!
Mutant overlord Apocalypse offers to remove **shrapnel** from Hulk's brain if he will serve him. Hulk agrees—and is turned into an **armored agent of destruction** named War, one of the villainous Horsemen of Apocalypse!

Justin Hammer hires Rhino to **kidnap** Bruce Banner, but he is **KNOCKED OUT** by the Green Giant!
Winner: Hulk!

The Leader **possesses** Rhino's **mind** and uses him to fight the Hulk – **IN SPACE!**
Winner: Hulk!

Rhino gets a job as a **shopping-mall Santa,** but is attacked by Hulk. **Winner: No one –** a little girl tells them to **STOP FIGHTING!**

ALTERNATE UNIVERSE

In an alternate world where the **Spider-Queen** rules Manhattan, the arachnid ruler turns the Hulk into one of her **creepy servants –** the bizarre **Spider-Hulk!**

SPIDER SMASH!

The Hulk signs up with a **pro baseball team** – but Rhino is playing for the **opposition** and they end up in **A BIG FIGHT.**
Winner: Hulk!

"If it's a war you truly desire, Thor—then Loki can happily provide."

BATTLING BROTHERS

Thor and **Loki** take brotherly rivalry to a **whole other level!** It's a power struggle between the heroic **God of Thunder** and the villainous **God of Mischief.** Who will win? **All bets are off!**

"You will pay for what you have done! NOTHING will save you!"

OUTNUMBERED!

Thor is cursed by Hela, Queen of Hel, to be immortal, but unable to heal. Loki sends every villain he can find after his brother – reducing him to an immortal puddle!

NOOOOO!!

Loki is **BANISHED**, but he wants to battle his brother. To bring Thor to him, he **TRICKS HULK** into causing a train wreck. Thor hunts the trickster down – and walks right into his trap!

NOOOOO!!

LOKI TRIES TO KILL

Loki manipulates Norman Osborn into son of hero Kevin Masterson. Furious, **THUNDERSTRIKE.** Thor drains Loki's life force – breaking Asgardian law and forcing Odin to **BANISH** his favourite son!

REDEMPTION

Loki manipulates Norman Osborn into leading an attack on Asgard. When the city is almost destroyed, Loki realises he has gone too far. He tries to help the Avengers, only to be killed by the hero Sentry's villainous alter-ego, the Void!

TOP 5

Ways to defeat LOKI

1 **ATTACK** him with thunder and lightning

2 **ASSEMBLE** the Avengers

3 **CONVINCE HIM** to fight without magic

4 **TELL ODIN** to force him to stop causing trouble

5 **TEAM UP** with a more powerful magician

TOP 5

Ways to defeat THOR

1 **TRICK HIM** with magic

2 **TELL ODIN** he's being a naughty boy

3 **ATTACK** while he's in one of his human forms

4 **TEAM UP** with a powerful Super Villain

5 **SEPARATE HIM** from his magical hammer, Mjolnir

THOR VS LOKI

THOR	LOKI
2m (6ft 6in)	1.9m (6ft 4in)
290kg (640lbs)	238kg (525lbs)
Asgardian	Frost Giant
Thunder & lightning	Powerful magic
Mjolnir & Belt of Strength	Norn Stones
Military skills	Cunning & trickery
Hand-to-hand combat	Illusions

Thor wins... providing he can get his hands on the trickster!

REALLY?!

Loki turns Thor into a **frog!** This doesn't stop Thor from **hopping all the way to Asgard** and putting Loki in his place!

KAPOW!

Loki creates multiple images of himself to fool Thor, but the Thunder God twirls Mjolnir at the speed of a propeller and blows all the phony Lokis off a cliff!

BAD DAY

Odin is tricked by Loki into banishing Thor from Asgard and taking half of his power away. Loki then gets villain the Tomorrow Man to attack the weakened Thunder God!

If you can't beat up your big brother, try enlisting someone else! The Power Cosmic! The with the Silver Surfer is trapped on Earth for eternity, so Loki offers to free him – if he destroys Thor!

TELL ME MORE!

The reason the brothers fall out is mainly Loki's fault – he's jealous that their father Odin and the other Asgardians like Thor more than him. Loki doesn't help by calling himself the God of Mischief!

WHAT YOU COULD DO WITH THE MANDARIN'S RINGS...

- Turn Iron Man into iron dust with **REMAKER**

- Crush enemies into the ground with **DAIMONIC**

- Keep meddling heroes at bay with **INFLUENCE**

- Turn up the heat with **INCANDESCENCE**

- Trap a foe in a tornado with **SPIN**

- Shock your friends with **LIGHTNING**

- Turn roadblocks to rubble with **SPECTRAL**

- Create illusions with The **LIAR**

- Keep everyone in the dark with **NIGHTBRINGER**

- Freeze foes solid with **ZERO**

WHAT?!

Mandarin wants machines to house the dangerous alien spirits in his rings, so he kidnaps Tony Stark to make them. Tony saves the world by convincing the Mandarin's minions that the Mandarin is insane with power.

DRAGON ALLY

With the help of Makluan dragon **Fin Fang Foom**, one of the Fantastic Four's **most threatening foes**, the Mandarin conquers a sizable chunk of **mainland China.**

TELL ME MORE!

Raised in poverty in China, the Mandarin ventures into the forbidden Valley of the Spirits, where he discovers an abandoned spaceship containing ten rings. They were forged by the dragon-like aliens of Maklu IV.

TONY'S A WINNER!

Despite the **MANDARIN'S WILES** and the **POWER OF HIS RINGS**, he never gets the better of **IRON MAN** for long! Maybe this Super Villain just tries **TOO HARD!**

When the Mandarin's hands are severed, he reintegrates his rings into his body by embedding them in his spine!

YECCH!

YESSS!! Mandarin has complete mastery over his **CHI,** or vital life-force. When imprisoned by the Chinese government, he survives without food or water – **FOR YEARS!**

BETWEEN...

The Mandarin is one of Tony's oldest foes, debuting in *Tales of Suspense* #50 (February 1964), one year after Iron Man premiered in the same title.

...THE PANELS

"I propose a duel, Iron Man. You against me, **ONE ON ONE.**"

BEHIND THE IRON MASK

Mandarin seeks to **destroy Stark Industries** for years before he discovers that Tony Stark is Iron Man. At one point, the Mandarin **rips off Iron Man's Faceplate** only to be **Fooled by a rubber mask!**

EXTREME MEASURES

Iron Man Tony Stark has a **big problem** when Mandarin seeks out scientist **Maya Hansen,** Tony's former girlfriend, and attempts to **eliminate** most of the world's population using her **Extremis technology.**

ALTERNATE UNIVERSE

In the **animal-filled alternate reality** of Spider-Ham, the Mandarin is a **ring-tailed lemur** known as **Mandaringtail!**

POWER STRUGGLE!

The Mandarin is Iron Man's **most persistent foe.** This evil genius doesn't go toe-to-toe with **ol' Shellhead** by suiting up in armour. His **ten rings** allow him vast control over **energy and matter!**

GRUDGE MATCH

Green Goblin Norman Osborn and his crazy Goblin dynasty are responsible for the **greatest tragedies** in **Peter Parker's life.** Spider-Man has overcome the Green Goblin **many times**, but there's always a **new Goblin** in town!

BAD DAY

Peter Parker is exposed to the **Goblin Formula** by Norman Osborn. Peter is the only person to resist the **formula's** madness... so far!

REALLY?!

The Green Goblin doesn't always want to **destroy** Spider-Man. Norman actually tries to **brainwash** Peter into becoming his **son!**

TROUBLE WITH HARRY

Norman Osborn's son **Harry** is Peter Parker's friend at university. Things turn sour when Harry **unfairly** blames Spider-Man for his father's death and becomes a **second Green Goblin** to avenge him.

WHEN BAD GUYS GO GOOD!

NEVER TOO LATE

Troubled Green Goblin Harry Osborn defeats Spider-Man and sets a bomb to blow them both up. M.J. arrives with Normie, Harry's little son, and Harry realises what he's done. He saves M.J., Normie and Spidey just before the bomb explodes!

TELL ME MORE!

Green Goblin Norman Osborn kidnaps Peter's girlfriend Gwen Stacy and throws her off a bridge. Spidey swears revenge and pursues the Green Goblin. In the fight that follows, the Goblin dies, accidentally impaled on his own Goblin Glider.

"You see, Parker? I always knew I could defeat you *ANY TIME* I wanted..."

AAAARRGHH!!!

Sometimes Spider-Man **LOSES** his battles. After the former **SCARLET SPIDER BEN REILLY** assumes the role of Spider-Man, he's killed by the Green Goblin.

TOP 5
Goblin Gadgets

PUMPKIN BOMBS
Exploding jack-o'-lanterns!

GOBLIN GLASSES
Mess with Spidey's senses!

GOBLIN GLOVES
Shoot blasts of Goblin sparks!

SONIC TOADS AND ELECTRIC FROGS
Little sound and energy bombs!

GOBLIN GLIDER
Smashes into people and fires lasers!

Q: Is Norman Osborn always evil?

A: No. When the Green Goblin is thrown against **electrical wiring** while fighting Spidey, the shock gives him **amnesia**. Norman **forgets** his villainous past and even **becomes kind!**

483
The top speed of the Green Goblin's glider in kph (300mph).

BEFORE

UPGRADED!
The Goblin Glider isn't the Goblin's first ride. He originally rode upon a rocket-powered broom!

AFTER

TOP 8
Goblins

1 **THE GREEN GOBLIN** – Norman Osborn, the first Green Goblin and inventor of the Goblin Formula.

2 **THE SECOND GREEN GOBLIN** – Harry Osborn continues his father Norman's legacy.

3 **THE THIRD GREEN GOBLIN** – Harry Osborn's psychiatrist, Bart Hamilton.

4 **THE HOBGOBLIN** – Roderick Kingsley follows Norman Osborn's journals to become the first of many evil Hobgoblins.

5 **THE FOURTH GREEN GOBLIN** and the **SIXTH HOBGOBLIN** – ex-journalist Phil Urich.

6 **MENACE** – Lily Hollister, the occasional girlfriend of both Norman and Harry Osborn.

7 **THE GREY GOBLIN** – Gabriel Stacy needs extra Goblin Formula injections to combat accelerated aging.

8 **CARLIE COOPER** – one of Peter Parker's girlfriends. She discovers a cure for the Goblin Formula!

NEVER-ENDING WAR

Liberty versus tyranny, freedom versus force, heroism versus hatred... **Captain America** and **the villainous Red Skull** have waged a **battle** between **good and evil ever since World War II** – and they don't look like **calling it quits** anytime soon!

UPGRADED!

The Red Skull creates Sleeper Robots for the Nazis after their defeat in World War II. He plans to join them together into one giant robot, travel to the North Pole and then explode the planet's core!

THOOM! THOOM! THOOM! THOOM!

NEVER TOO OLD!

When the Red Skull's **aging process accelerates**, he uses a poison to make Captain America age, too – hoping to **take Cap to the grave with him!** With only hours to live, Cap **defeats Skull** in hand-to-hand combat – giving him time to find a cure, while **Red Skull dies of old age!**

Red Skull re-creates a powerful **Cosmic Cube** that can alter the fabric of reality – and uses it to **swap bodies with Cap!**

"I damn you Captain America for what you are! We are DEADLY OPPOSITES you and I..."

"You *HAVEN'T BEATEN ME* yet, Skull!"

MASTER OF DISGUISE

The Red Skull becomes U.S. Secretary of State under the alias **Dell Rusk.** He plots to release a biological weapon, the **Red Zone Plague,** at Mount Rushmore. Once again, it's a race against time for Cap to foil yet another nefarious plan!

YEESS!!

When Cap is **CAPTURED** by the Red Skull, the Skull's ally, villainous computer wiz and robotics expert **MACHINESMITH,** downloads all of Cap's memories – and uses them to **FRAME CAP FOR TREASON!**

WHEN GOOD GUYS GO BAD!

TELEVISION TROUBLE

To save New York from the Red Skull's diabolical plans, Captain America vows to serve the villain for one day! His promise is secretly televised, and Cap is branded a traitor!

ALTERNATE UNIVERSE

In the **Ultimate Universe (Earth-1610),** the Red Skull is not a World War II enemy of Captain America, but **his own son!** After his father's death, he is **raised and trained** on an army base to **succeed Steve Rogers,** but instead he becomes the villainous Red Skull!

BACK FROM THE DEAD?

At the end of World War II, Cap and Skull **battle in Hitler's bunker** – and the Red Skull is **seemingly killed** by a cave-in! An experimental gas keeps Skull alive for decades in **suspended animation,** and he returns **more evil than ever!**

REAL NAME: Wilson Fisk, alias Kingpin

OCCUPATION: crime boss

SKILLS: sumo wrestling, martial arts, but usually relies on henchmen to do his dirty work

"We need each other, Daredevil... *WE* are the power in this city."

BAD DAY

Fisk uses his knowledge of Matt Murdock's **secret identity** to expose Daredevil to the F.B.I., but his **trumped-up** evidence against Murdock **backfires** and lands them both in jail!

BETWEEN...

Hell's Kitchen is a real-life area of New York City once notorious for crime and violence. It first appears in the Marvel Universe in *Daredevil #1* (April 1964).

...THE PANELS

ONLY

WHO BEATS WHO?

DAREDEVIL

HEIGHT: 1.9m (6ft)

WEIGHT: 91kg (200lbs)

STRENGTHS:
Superhuman senses, martial arts, legal eagle

KINGPIN

HEIGHT: 2.1m (6ft 7in)

WEIGHT: 204kg (450lbs)

STRENGTHS:
Sumo wrestling skills, legions of henchmen, powerful connections

Despite Kingpin's considerable size and weight advantage, we're going to have to call this one a **draw!**

AAAARRGHH!!

Daredevil's on-off girlfriend, **KAREN PAGE**, reveals Daredevil's identity to **KINGPIN** who uses the knowledge to make the hero's life a **NIGHTMARE!**

DOUBLE TROUBLE

MURDOCK & FISK

Matt Murdock and Wilson Fisk are both cooling their heels in Ryker's Island prison when they realise that outside forces are trying to pit them against each other. With Bullseye's help, Fisk breaks himself and Murdock out of jail to battle those responsible!

TRAGEDY!

Matt Murdock's college sweetheart, **Elektra**, goes bad and works as an assassin for Kingpin. When she refuses to kill Matt's law partner and friend, **Foggy Nelson**, she is murdered by Kingpin's henchman **Bullseye**. This incident fuels Matt's **hatred** for Kingpin for years.

BEST KNOWN FOR

FIGHTING IN COURT AND ON THE STREETS

KITCHEN DEVILS!

The two most powerful influences in New York City's Hell's Kitchen are Daredevil, Matt Murdock and gang boss the Kingpin, Wilson Fisk. They battle for control of their turf, one hoping to protect it, and the other to control it.

HEARTBREAKER!

If you want to **destroy your enemy,** start with their **heart!** Wilson Fisk gets nutty psychic **Typhoid Mary** to romance Matt Murdock and then **dump him.**

AAAARRGHH!!

The monstrous **ABOMINATION** holds his own against Hulk, but he's no match for the ruthless **RED HULK**! The scarlet giant shoots him with a special gun designed to **KILL HULKS!**

Power Up!

HOTHEAD!
When the **RED HULK** gets angry, he doesn't get stronger – he gets **HOTTER**! If he's angry enough he can **MELT THINGS** around him and fire **HEAT BLASTS** from his eyes!

ATOMIC POWER!
Rick Jones is a **faithful sidekick** to the Hulk, Mar-Vell and Captain America, but after the **Intelligencia** transform him into an **Abomination-like monster** named **A-Bomb**, he stops being so helpful!

YESSS!!

RED HULK declares himself the **RULER OF THE U.S.A.**, so **THE HULK** knocks him down to size and off his feet with a huge **THUNDER-CLAP!** Green Hulks really are **THE BEST!**

S.H.I.E.L.D. DECLASSIFIED

THE TRANSFORMATIONS OF BETTY ROSS
Bruce Banner's ex-wife Betty Ross is transformed twice by gamma radiation. First she is turned into the winged and wicked Harpy by the evil M.O.D.O.K. Later, after she dies, the Leader uses gamma rays to bring her back as the furious Red She-Hulk.

REALLY?!

Like his Biblical namesake, super-shrink **Doc Samson** draws his power from his **hair**! The longer his **gamma-green** locks grow, the **stronger** he becomes!

ALL-NEW HULK
Amadeus Cho is already a teenage **super genius**, but when a rampaging **sea monster** interrupts his day at the beach, he reveals his **all-new** super-powered gamma form – and becomes the **totally awesome Hulk!**

HULKS SMASH!

The Incredible Hulk isn't the only **muscle-bound monster** created by gamma radiation – there's a **whole family** of bizarre beings you really **don't want to make angry!**

SHE-HULK
Bruce Banner's cousin Jen Walters

RED SHE-HULK
Bruce's former wife, Betty Ross

RED-HULK
Betty's father and Hulk's enemy, General Thaddeus "Thunderbolt" Ross

WOW!

384,400

The distance Red Hulk can cover in a single bound, in km (238,835 miles). He once jumped all the way to Earth from the moon!

SAVAGE SHE-HULK
Hulk's daughter Lyra from an alternate future

SKARR
Hulk's long-lost son

BRAINSTORM
Gamma radiation causes Samuel Sterns to turn into the Leader – a criminal super-genius with a huge skull and gamma-powered brain. He tries to up his intelligence and brain size even more, but his experiments mutate him into a giant monster!

BEFORE...

...AFTER

SMASH BROTHERS
The Hulk clan **have their differences,** but when they're faced with the menace of **gamma-powered dragon Fin Fang Foom,** the Hulk, Red She-Hulk, A-Bomb and She-Hulk agree on one thing: it's time to **smash back!**

TITANIC TUSSLE

In the **red corner,** the fearless felon with a **big heart,** and **even bigger fists** – Titania!
In the **green corner,** the mean, muscular hero with **a heck of a temper** – She-Hulk!
Let battle commence!

BEST OF ENEMIES

Titania and the **Absorbing Man** get revenge on **She-Hulk** by infecting her with **mind-controlling microscopic nanites!** Now under their control, She-Hulk joins her enemies on a **rampage through New York!**

WINNER: TITANIA

S.H.I.E.L.D. DECLASSIFIED

TITANIA
Mary "Skeeter" MacPherran is an unpopular teen who dreams of being a glamorous Super Hero. When she is kidnapped to Battleworld during the Secret Wars, Dr Doom offers to give her superpowers – and she becomes the mighty villainess Titania, obsessed with proving she's stronger than She-Hulk!

GRUDGE MATCH

KRASH!

LUCKY ESCAPE
In their very first fight on Battleworld, Titania knocks She-Hulk down, then gets loads of other villains to help finish the heroine off while she is helpless! If Shulkie's friends hadn't burst in to save her, she would've been a goner!
Winner: **TITANIA** *(but she cheated!)*

Power Up!

BREAKER OF MEN
In order to cause chaos and destruction, Asgardian villain the **SERPENT** summons the seven hammers of the worthy to Earth. Titania picks one up and becomes the mighty **SKIRN, BREAKER OF MEN!**

DOUBLE DATE!

Luke Cage

Absorbing Man

Titania and the **Absorbing Man** try to rob **a fancy restaurant**, but they bump into She-Hulk on a dinner date with **Luke Cage**. The couples fight, and the Absorbing Man accidentally **knocks Titania out** with his whirling ball and chain!

Winner: SHE-HULK!

"It's not the first blow that counts. It's the **LAST.**"

BETWEEN...

She-Hulk works at the Goodman, Lieber, Kurtzberg and Holliway law firm. Martin Goodman, Stan Lee (formerly Lieber) and Jack Kirby (formerly Kurtzberg) are three legends of Marvel!

...THE PANELS

A KNOCKOUT BLOW

Titania gets the Infinity Gem of Power from the Champion of the Universe, enabling her to beat She-Hulk with ease. Shulkie turns back into Jen Walters to escape, steals the Gem – and knocks Titania out with a single punch!

WINNER: SHE-HULK!

COURT IN THE ACT!

She-Hulk is in the **U.S. Supreme Court**, arguing against the **Mutant Registration Act**, but Titania keeps causing trouble outside! In fact, she's spoiling for a fight! She-Hulk **clobbers her three times** – while managing to **keep track** of the legal proceedings!

WINNER: SHE-HULK!

Power Up!

HULKING UP

When Jen Walters becomes **SHE-HULK**, her strength grows accordingly. Shulkie can usually lift 100 tons, but after some **SERIOUS TRAINING**, she gets strong enough to beat **HERCULES** in an arm-wrestle!

TELL ME MORE!

Lawyer Jennifer Walters is shot by a gang she is prosecuting in court, and her quick-thinking cousin, Bruce Banner, saves her life with a transfusion of his own gamma-radiated blood. Jen soon discovers that she can hulk out, too. But unlike Bruce, she remains intelligent when she changes into She-Hulk!

RESULT!

SHE-HULK: 3
TITANIA: 2

TELL ME MORE!

Atlantis, ruled by Namor the Sub-Mariner, is a sunken city the size of a small continent located somewhere in the Atlantic Ocean. It is home to the Atlanteans – a bluish cousin of humans who are able to breath underwater – but is coveted by the savage Mermen of Lemuria, led by Attuma.

WHO BEATS WHOM?

Don't let Attuma's **massive physique** fool you – the bigger they come, the harder they fall, and the **faster they sink!** While these guys are fairly evenly matched in fighting skills, **Namor** can **battle on** for far longer. Couple this with his ability to fly, and the Sub-Mariner is a **likely winner!**

"So long as Namor stands Atlantis shall be denied you-- FOREVER!"

TOP 6

How to Rule Atlantis

1 **GATHER** a ruthless Mermen army

2 **ENSLAVE** Atlanteans with hypnotic lights

3 **INFILTRATE** the Atlantean government

4 **FORCE** Namor to surrender by holding the surface world hostage

5 **STEAL** an unstoppable alien robot

6 **FIND** an enchanted hammer that gives you superpowers

BETWEEN...

Namor and Attuma have been battling each other for more than 50 years! The malevolent Merman first appears in *Fantastic Four #33* (December 1964), when his barbarian hordes invade Atlantis.

...THE PANELS

DUEL IN THE DEEP

AAARRGHH!!

ATTUMA creates an evil alliance with **TIGER SHARK** and **DR DORCAS**. Namor takes on all three; he **LOSES** and is taken prisoner.

HANDLE WITH CARE!

Attuma finds an **ancient magical hammer** and becomes **Nerkkod, Breaker of Oceans.** He conquers the waves, destroys Atlantis and finally **defeats Namor!**

"**DEATH TO SUB-MARINER!!** Only Attuma will wear the crown of Atlantis!!"

YESSS!! Using **BRUCE BANNER'S BLOOD,** Attuma **GAMMA-RADIATES HIMSELF** and captures Atlantis – until Namor gets Hulk to **SMASH ATTUMA** back to normal!

GOOD DAY

When **Attuma attacks Atlantis,** Namor's girlfriend, **Lady Dorma,** begs the **Fantastic Four** for help. They **hold off the Mermen army,** allowing Namor to **defeat Attuma,** but keep their presence a **secret** – Namor's **big ego** can't handle his sometime enemies **saving his gills!**

Namor the Sub-Mariner and his **archenemy Attuma** wrestle for control of the submerged **City of Atlantis.** The **massive Merman** will do **whatever it takes** to depose King Namor and finally **rule the oceans!**

Q: What makes Mermen and Atlanteans different?

A: Both can **breathe underwater** and have **bluish skin.** Mermen look more fishlike and are **more barbaric.** Atlantean society is **more advanced** – politically, scientifically and **magically.**

Atlanteans

Merman

HEAVY HITTERS

If one of this bunch hits you, you're **not getting up!** Most heroes and villains **pack a powerful punch,** but these folks are the **biggest bashers** and the **most thunderous thumpers** around!

AAAARRGHH!!

HULK can beat heavy hitters like the Thing, Thor and Wolverine, but even he's been **KNOCKED BACK!** When Spider-Man is imbued with the **POWER COSMIC,** he punches Hulk **INTO ORBIT!**

HULK BUSTING

If you want a crack at **Tony Stark,** you better make sure he's not wearing his **Hulkbuster armour.** With it, Shellhead can lift **175 tons** – it's made to **bust Hulks,** after all!

TOUGH STUFF

Hulk tries to rescue his friend **Rick Jones** from the **Wrecker.** However, a misunderstanding puts him on a **collision course** with the **Fantastic Four** – and an **epic showdown** with fellow power-puncher, **the Thing!**

Power Up!

COMING THROUGH!

A gem from the magical **CYTTORAK** turns Cain Marko into the nearly indestructible **JUGGERNAUT.** This human battering ram is super-strong and can **CRUSH MOUNTAINS!**

TELL ME MORE!

Heavy-hitters Thor and Hercules are good friends, but also rivals. While they both wield a mean weapon with mighty strength, Herc just can't keep up with Thor's god-given speed and lightning blasts!

YESSS!!

The Midgard Serpent wraps its planet-sized body all the way around the Earth, but **Thor** is so strong that he removes it – with a **fishing rod!**

S.H.I.E.L.D. DECLASSIFIED

CAPTAIN MARVEL
Captain Marvel Carol Danvers' superstrength is matched only by her iron will. Her ability to absorb energy means that the more power that is thrown at her, the stronger her next attack becomes.

REALLY?!

Molly Hayes is just a little kid, but she can **punch** so hard she once sent Wolverine **flying through a wall.** No wonder they call her **Bruiser,** though she prefers the name **Princess Powerful!**

WHEN GOOD GUYS GO BAD

EVIL INSIDE
Sentry (Bob Reynolds) is created by an improved version of the Super-Soldier serum that transformed Steve Rogers into Captain America. He has the power of one million exploding suns, but has a dark side named the Void, who destroys the city of Asgard!

THICK-SKINNED HERO
Piotr Rasputin is a **nice guy** with a **hard exterior.** When the going gets tough, he becomes the hero **Colossus** – a member of **the X-Men** with the power to convert his body tissue into **organic steel**.

UPGRADED!

Rhino isn't big on brains, but this musclebound Russian science experiment doesn't care. His superpowered suit makes him almost invulnerable – and it's bonded to him for life!

BACK FROM THE DEAD!

Wonder Man is living ionic energy! He's as strong as they come and **can't feel pain** – which is just as well as he has **died several times!**

TOP 4

Reasons Thor Fights Hercules

1 Herc hits on Thor's girlfriend **JANE FOSTER**

2 Herc joins up with the evil god **PLUTO**

3 Herc and Thor argue over a **MAGIC PIG**

4 They both want to **CROSS A BRIDGE FIRST**

1. SHANG-CHI – it takes a lot to break Shang-Chi's state of Zen calm, but if you do, watch out!

2. ELEKTRA – swaps life as a deadly assassin-for-hire to fight crime alongside Daredevil

3. IRON FIST – martial arts master who possesses the ancient power of the Iron Fist

4. KARNAK – a warrior monk who has trained to the point of Inhuman physical perfection

5. DAREDEVIL – trained by the legendary Stick to fight the underworld bosses of Hell's Kitchen, New York City

Power Up!

HARD HITTER
DANIEL RAND (Iron Fist) gains his greatest power in a **SPECIAL RITUAL**. He slays the dragon **SHUO-LAO THE UNDYING** and then plunges his hands into its **MOLTEN HEART** – imbuing them with the hard-hitting mystic power of **IRON FIST!**

FISTS OF FURY

Patience, hard work and **dedication** can transform body and mind into an **ultimate fighting machine.** These **masters of martial arts** may not all have superpowers, but mess with them and they will **take you down!**

UPGRADED!

Karnak utilises the **superhuman strength** all **Inhumans** are born with by studying **martial arts**. Instead of gaining more powers through the **Terrigen Mists** like other Inhumans, he trains until he can shatter objects with **a single blow!**

WHEN BAD GUYS GO GOOD!

UNLIKELY ALLIES

Martial arts master Cat (Shen Kuei) believes that Shang-Chi caused his brother's death. When he learns this is not so, Cat teams up with Shang-Chi to take down those actually responsible – Cat's former criminal allies!

MASTER OF KUNG FU

Shang-Chi is the **ultimate martial arts master**. His crime lord father raises him to be a **ruthless assassin,** but the plan backfires. The Kung Fu warrior **swears vengeance,** battling crime as Earth's most **skilful fighter!**

NOOOOO!! **ELEKTRA** is trained by **STICK,** an enemy of the evil **HAND NINJA**. Stick does not allow Elektra to finish her training – so she **JOINS** the Hand instead!

HEROES FOR HIRE

Iron Fist and **Luke Cage** decide to go into business together as **"Heroes for Hire"**. They plan to help people and make money, but the pair often end up doing heroic deeds **for free!**

ALTERNATE UNIVERSE

In the **Mangaverse** (Earth-2301), Peter Parker is not a student and photographer – he's the **last ninja** of the ancient **Spider Clan!** He seeks revenge on **Venom,** the monster who killed his sensei, **Uncle Ben!**

TOP 5

Shang-Chi Versus...

How does the Master of Kung Fu match up against superpowered opponents?

1 **WOLVERINE** – Wolvie is trying to control his rage, but gets angry, fights Shang-Chi and loses!

2 **SPIDER-MAN** – a misunderstanding leads to a fight, but the pair quickly call a truce.

3 **THING** – Shang-Chi withstands all of the Thing's attacks, then refuses to fight back!

4 **CAPTAIN AMERICA** – both Shang-Chi and Cap land hits, but neither of these tough guys go down!

5 **MAN-THING** – Shang-Chi gets trapped inside the muddy monster!

BACK FROM THE DEAD!

Iron Fist is **murdered** and his crime-fighting partner **Luke Cage** is blamed. However, the victim is actually an **alien double** and the real Iron Fist returns to **clear Luke's name!**

CHAPTER TWO
TEAMS

Wolverine is **MUCH OLDER** than he seems – but what keeps him looking so young?

Who kills **UATU THE WATCHER** and steals his eye?

What turns **MADAME HYDRA** into a humanoid octopus creature?

SUPER HERO TEAMS

EARTH'S MIGHTIEST!

The Avengers are always facing some big new problem! They've been disassembled, reassembled and nearly obliterated. They've even fought each other. Yet they regroup each time a Super Villain threatens the future of humanity!

KEY MEMBERS:
Iron Man, Thor, Ant-Man (Henry Pym), The Wasp, Hulk, Captain America, Hawkeye, Vision, Scarlet Witch, Quicksilver, Black Panther, Black Widow, Falcon, Winter Soldier, Hercules, Black Knight, She-Hulk, Ant-Man (Scott Lang), Wonder Man, Quasar, Spectrum

ALLIES: Rick Jones, Edwin Jarvis, Nick Fury, Nick Fury Jr, Fantastic Four, S.H.I.E.L.D.

ENEMIES: Ultron, Kang, Masters of Evil, Thanos, Baron Zemo, Loki and many, many more!

TOP 8

Times Avengers HQ has been wrecked!

1 **THE MASTERS OF EVIL** invade Avengers Mansion and **TRASH** the place!

2 The Avengers move to **HYDROBASE**, an artificial island off the coast of New Jersey, but attacking robots sink it!

3 The team's rebuilt mansion is **TRASHED AGAIN** – this time by the extradimensional **GATHERERS**!

4 **SCARLET WITCH**, **VISION** and **JACK OF HEARTS** go out of control, and the mansion is wrecked!

5 The team moves into **STARK TOWER**, but it's wrecked when **IRON MAN** and **HULK** clash!

6 An Asgardian-empowered **THING** wrecks the tower again, battling **RED HULK**!

7 A new Avengers team moves into a rebuilt **AVENGERS MANSION**, but it's wrecked yet again when **POWER MAN** attacks!

8 **THE CHILDREN OF TOMORROW** from Earth-1610 **SMASH** a rebuilt Stark Tower!

Iron Man

Captain America

Thor

"We'll never be beaten! For we are... the AVENGERS!"

Nova

Spider-Man

KAPOW!
Ant-Man likes to give Hawkeye's arrows an added punch – by hitching a ride!

BROKEN HEART
Wasp Janet Van Dyne is the **heart** of the Avengers. She **names** the group, **chairs** their first meeting and **holds** the group together, even when her husband, **Hank Pym,** cracks up.

Ms Marvel

WHEN GOOD GUYS GO BAD!

ROBO-SPIDEY
When Spider-Man meets the Avengers for the first time, he's an evil webhead – a robot created by Kang the Conqueror sent to destroy them!

Q: What is the Avengers Academy?
A: The Avengers establish the **Avengers Academy** to train super-powered students to become **heroes,** rather than the **villains** they might otherwise become!

LOYAL SERVANT
Edwin Jarvis is the **butler** of **Tony Stark** and the **Avengers.** His loyalty is unwavering – even when he's **beaten senseless** by **Mister Hyde** or **replaced** by a Skrull invader!

BETWEEN...
When the first issue of *Daredevil* was delayed, Stan Lee suggested Marvel release a team-up title. *The Avengers #1* debuted in September 1963, and the rest is history!

...THE PANELS

NOOOOO!!
She-Hulk doesn't often lose her temper like her cousin Hulk, but when her Avengers teammate Vision is taken over by Ultron and attacks the group, she loses control – and literally tears him apart!

Vision

AAARGHH!!
A **BASEMENT DOOR** in Avengers Mansion turns out to be a **PORTAL** for Kang the Conqueror to **INVADE** the world!

127

When **trouble comes calling,** there's an **Avengers team** ready for action – **any time, any place, anywhere!**

TOP **5** AVENGERS TEAMS

1 **PET AVENGERS** – a team of super animals

2 **GREAT LAKES AVENGERS** – a collection of America's weirdest heroes

3 **DARK AVENGERS** – Norman Osborn's squad of crooks and murderers

4 **UNCANNY AVENGERS** – a team of mutants and Super Heroes

5 **WEST COAST AVENGERS** – sworn to battle any threat, so long as it's west of the Rockies!

Uncanny Avengers

S.H.I.E.L.D. DECLASSIFIED

SECRET AVENGERS
A secret team is created to serve S.H.I.E.L.D.'s black ops interests. Led by Nick Fury Jr., the team includes Hawkeye, Black Widow, Spider-Woman, Agent Phil Coulson and, bizarrely, the giant-headed evil genius M.O.D.O.K.!

ALTERNATE UNIVERSE

The main Avengers are reincarnated as **Western heroes** in 1872. Steve Rogers is sheriff of the town of Timely, and Tony Stark is a blacksmith with a drinking problem!

Lockheed

Throg

Redwing

Hairball

Zabu

Ms Lion

CREATURE CRUSADERS

The Inhumans' watchdog **Lockjaw** gains telepathy and extra intelligence from the **Mind Gem**. He contacts heroes' pets and forms the **Pet Avengers** team!

Lockjaw

PURRRFECT PET AVENGERS

HAIRBALL – Speedball's super-powered feline can bounce off walls!

LOCKJAW – who can resist the big slobbery mug of the Inhumans' teleporting pooch?

THROG – he's a frog AND an honorary God of Thunder!

REDWING – he's just as slick as his human partner Falcon.

MS LION – Ms Lion is actually male and a normal, friendly little dog belonging to Peter Parker's Aunt May.

LOCKHEED – Kitty Pryde of the X-Men's super-powered alien dragon.

ZABU – Ka-Zar's faithful Savage Land companion. Who says that sabre-toothed tigers are extinct?!

TOP 6

GREAT LAKES AVENGERS

1 **SQUIRREL GIRL** – realises the lazy team are relying on her, and quits!

2 **MR. IMMORTAL** – able to survive almost any accident

3 **FLATMAN** – super-stretchy, but falls a bit flat

4 **ASHLEY CRAWFORD** – a supermodel who morphs into super-sized, super-strong Big Bertha

5 **DINAH SOAR** – a weird flying creature who loves Mr. Immortal

6 **DOORMAN** – a living portal into the Darkforce

Monkey Joe

Squirrel Girl

BETWEEN...

Great Lakes Avengers writer Dan Slott promised that a team member would die each issue, as a parody of overdone comic book deaths. The first to go: Squirrel Girl's squirrel buddy, Monkey Joe!

...THE PANELS

50,000

The number of years into the future the Avengers travel to meet the team's final incarnation.

TELL ME MORE!

The West Coast Avengers disperse, but many years later Hank Pym, Tigra and Hawkeye return to the team's LA headquarters to create Avengers Academy, for teen would-be heroes.

AAARRGHH!!
HAWKEYE founded the West Coast Avengers alongside Mockingbird, Wonder Man, Tigra and Jim Rhodes, but they just couldn't get along and were **BROKEN UP** by Captain America.

NOOOOO!!
When Norman Osborn becomes U.S. security chief he forms a Dark Avengers team of **SUPER VILLAINS!** Osborn is **IRON PATRIOT**, a devious combination of Iron Man and Captain America.

MUTANT MARVELS

The X-Men are a team of **mutants** united by **Professor Charles Xavier's** dream of **peaceful coexistence** with ordinary folks. They protect a world that sometimes **hates and fears** them, while safeguarding the future of the **endangered mutant race!**

Cyclops

THE ORIGINAL X-MEN

The roster soon grows, but the first students to enroll at Professor Xavier's School for Gifted Youngsters are:

- **CYCLOPS** (Scott Summers) – continually shoots force beams from eyes

- **MARVEL GIRL** (Jean Grey) – vast telepathic and telekinetic abilities

- **ANGEL** (Warren Worthington III) – flies like a bird

- **BEAST** (Henry McCoy) – ape-like genius scientist

- **ICEMAN** (Robert Drake) – transforms into ice; can freeze moisture in the air.

Q: WHAT IS A MUTANT?

A: A person born with a **genetic "x-factor"** that gives him or her **abilities** far beyond those of a normal human being. These powers often appear in **sudden and disturbing ways** during the teenage years.

Beast

Nightcrawler

FAST FACTS

KEY MEMBERS:
Professor X, Storm, Jean Grey, Nightcrawler, Colossus, Magik, Iceman, Wolverine, Angel, Beast, Cyclops, Emma Frost, Kitty Pryde

RELATED TEAMS: X-Force, Magneto's Uncanny X-Men

ALLIES: New Mutants, Fantastic Four, Spider-Man

TOP 5

UNFORTUNATE MUTANTS

1 **ROGUE** – absorbs the memories and abilities of anyone she touches, leaving them in a coma!

2 **NIGHTCRAWLER** – a swashbuckling and loyal X-Man, but shunned as a child for his demonic appearance

3 **MAGGOTT** – eats through two slug-like creatures that gobble up food and burrow into his body!

4 **SNOT** – a teenage villain who generates deadly mucus from his oversized nostrils!

5 **BEAST** – Hank McCoy's science experiments have left him with fangs, claws and thick blue fur

WHOSE SIDE ARE THEY ON?

- **Magneto** – the master of magnetism hates humans, but when all mutants are in danger, he becomes a vital X-Men ally!
- **Gambit** – this master thief is both an X-Man and a criminal!
- **Emma Frost** – this diamond-skinned telepath realises the X-Men aren't so bad when Sentinel robots attack her people on the mutant haven of Genosha.
- **Jean Grey** – a cosmic force turns her into the world-destroying Dark Phoenix!

AAAARRGHH!!

CYCLOPS cannot control the **FORCE BEAMS** that shoot from his **EYES**. He has to wear a **RUBY-QUARTZ VISOR**, or destroy anything he looks at!

Colossus

Emma Frost

WOW!

100
...and counting

Wolverine's age, but you wouldn't know it, thanks to his amazing healing factor.

"I'm the best there is at what I do, but what I do best isn't very nice."

Wolverine

TOP 5
X-MEN ENEMIES

1 **APOCALYPSE** – his name says it all. This ancient mutant wants to rule the world, or destroy it!

2 **SABRETOOTH** – big, mean, furry and full of fury, Sabretooth has only one goal: slay Wolverine!

3 **MR. SINISTER** – genetic manipulator with a cruel streak and an obsession with mutant DNA; a modern-day mad scientist!

4 **MYSTIQUE** – wicked, shape-changing schemer related to Nightcrawler and Rogue

5 **JUGGERNAUT** – nothing stops Xavier's half brother, the super-strong, nigh-invulnerable Juggernaut!

FASTBALL SPECIAL
When Wolverine wants to **slice'n'dice** something **far away** he pops his **claws** and gets his big buddy **Colossus** to **chuck him** at the target!

FAST FACTS

MEMBERS: Mister Fantastic (Reed Richards), Human Torch (Johnny Storm), Invisible Woman (Susan Richards), The Thing (Ben Grimm).

BASE: Baxter Building, New York City

ALLIES: Agatha Harkness, Alicia Masters, Lyja Storm, Silver Surfer, Wyatt Wingfoot.

FOES: Doctor Doom, Frightful Four, Wizard, Mole Man, Puppet Master, Red Ghost (and his Super Apes), Klaw

Q: How do the Fantastic Four get superhuman powers?

A: Reed Richards, his girlfriend Susan Storm, her brother Johnny and pilot Ben Grimm make a **test flight** in an **experimental rocket**. The rocket is bombarded by **cosmic radiation** and crashes! The four emerge with amazing **new abilities!**

GOOD DAY

Doctor Doom tries to ruin Reed and Sue's wedding with his **Emotion Changer** machine, but the **Watcher** gives Reed a device to foil Doom's plan, **saving the day!**

YESSS!! The **FRIGHTFUL FOUR** bad guys are fleeing in their spaceship. Mr Fantastic becomes a giant **SPRING** and he **HURLS** Thing onto the ship for some **CLOBBERIN'!**

WOW!

457

Maximum length in metres Mr Fantastic can extend a body part (1,500ft).

MISTER FANTASTIC

ALTERNATE UNIVERSE

In the **Ultimate Universe** (Earth-1610), Mr Fantastic **goes insane!** He **fakes** his own death and sends **aliens** to attack his former friends! Battling Nova and Sue Richards, he ends up exiled to the **Negative Zone.**

"Family isn't just who you're related to—It's who cares for you and takes care of you."

INVISIBLE WOMAN

THE HUMAN TORCH

SUPER HERO FAMILY!

Transformed by cosmic rays, the **Fantastic Four** could have become **outcasts**. Instead they see their strange **new powers** as a family bond, and use them for **the good of humanity**! Mister Fantastic is famous for his **scientific genius**, but all four have become **celebrity heroes!**

WHEN GOOD GUYS go BAD!

THING'S RAMPAGE

A Reed Richards experiment turns the Thing back into Ben Grimm. What's more, Ben can change back whenever he wants. However, Ben's personality changes. He breaks up with his girlfriend, Alicia, quits the FF and rampages through New York City!

BETWEEN...

The Fantastic Four's November 1961 launch was a turning point for writer/editor Stan Lee, who had considered leaving comics. The FF have gone on to sell more than 150 million comic books.

...THE PANELS

NOOOOO!! Kristoff Vernard, a child brainwashed to think he's **DOCTOR DOOM**, traps the FF in the Baxter Building, shoots it into outer space and **BLOWS IT UP!**

COSMIC EFFECTS

Mister Fantastic: Reed's body becomes elastic, stretching in amazing ways!

Invisible Woman: Sue's new abilities include projecting force-fields and turning invisible!

Human Torch: Johnny gains the ability to fly, throw fireballs, bathe his body in flames, and the catchphrase, "Flame on!"

The Thing: Ben gains superhuman strength, a rock body and the catchphrase, "It's clobberin' time!"

UPGRADED!

Super Hero teams need super-fast transportation, so Reed designs the Fantasti-car. He soon upgrades his initial "flying bathtub" design to a machine that can split into four vehicles.

TOP 4
Fantastic Powers

1. **THE HUMAN TORCH** – can create flaming images of himself; an enemy has to figure out which one is **the real** Johnny Storm!

2. **MR FANTASTIC** – his body is so bendy it can even absorb the impacts of **artillery shells**.

3. **INVISIBLE WOMAN** – can create see-through, but solid, objects with her mind, such as vehicles and weapons.

4. **THE THING** – can withstand armour-piercing shells, extreme heat and cold and survive in space and the depths of the ocean.

TERRIGENESIS
Inhumans look just like normal humans, until they are exposed to mutagenic mists from the rare Terrigen crystals – a process known as "terrigenesis". Their bodies mutate inside large green cocoons, before they emerge with unique superhuman powers.

HOME SWEET HOME
The Inhumans' home is the city of **Attilan.** It's been located in **the Himalayas,** the blue area of the Moon, and even **levitating** above New York's **Hudson River** – but it's always home!

BETWEEN...
The Inhumans are no newbies! Medusa debuted in *Fantastic Four* #36, way back in 1965! Her origin story and fellow Inhumans were revealed later that year in *Fantastic Four* #45.

...THE PANELS

HANDLE WITH CARE!
Terrigen crystals create powerful mists that **unlock** Inhuman powers. The mists transform those with Inhuman genes, but can **kill** humans.

AAARRGHH!!
A **TERRIGEN BOMB** explodes on Earth! Carriers of the Inhuman gene are **FORCED** into Terrigenesis. These new Inhumans become known as **"NUHUMANS".**

TELL ME MORE!
A superpower derived from Terrigenesis can have seriously bad side effects. Any physical change is irreversible, so fingers crossed you get a good one!

Quick Wedding
Not every Inhuman wants to **marry** another Inhuman. Medusa's sister **Crystal** dates the **Human Torch** (Johnny Storm), then marries super-speedster **Quicksilver!**

WHEN GOOD GUYS
...THEN GOOD AGAIN!
Medusa loses her memory, joins up with the Frightful Four and battles the Fantastic Four! Eventually, she remembers who she is, and joins her former foes in a new team, the Future Foundation!

1 **BLACK BOLT** – king with an earth shattering voice and the ability to manipulate energy

2 **MEDUSA** – queen who can control her long red hair as a whip, to bind people, or lift objects

3 **MAXIMUS THE MAD** – brother of Black Bolt with psionic abilities but questionable sanity

4 **CRYSTAL** – sister of Medusa and ex-wife of Quicksilver; can manipulate earth, air, fire and water

5 **LOCKJAW** – looks like a dog; can teleport

6 **MS. MARVEL (KAMALA KHAN)** – can morph in size, shape, density and appearance

THANE

FAMILY CONNECTIONS

Thane, son of **Thanos** the Mad Titan, is revealed to be of **Inhuman lineage.** After his terrigenesis, the once kind doctor finds he can create **living death** with a touch of his hand – a power he uses to lock his evil father in **suspended animation!**

Power Up!

BLACK BOLT A **WHISPER** from the super-powered voice of **BLACK BOLT**, King of the Inhumans, can level an **ENTIRE CITY**. His terrigenesis took place **EARLIER** than any other Inhuman's, making his powers the **MOST DEVELOPED** of the entire race.

THE SUPER IN HUMANS

The Inhumans are a reclusive, genetically enhanced **super race.** Thousands of years ago, the alien **Kree** abducted cavemen and **experimented on them.** They hoped to build **an army,** but instead created an **entire race** of superhumans!

TROUBLESHOOTERS!

TELL ME MORE!

When Arthur Douglas' wife is killed by Thanos, he is genetically engineered to become Drax the Destroyer, the ultimate warrior with one aim – to destroy the mad Titan!

Drax the Destroyer

BETWEEN...

When they aren't busy saving the universe, the Guardians like to relax at Starlin's Bar on Knowhere – named for legendary artist and writer Jim Starlin, who worked on many of Marvel's cosmic comics!

...THE PANELS

Q: How did the Guardians of the Galaxy start?

A: When the **Kree homeworld** is attacked by the alien **Phalanx**, the Kree send a team of **expendable troopers** to fight back. Star-Lord leads a bizarre **group of convicts** who save the day. They then decide to stick together as a **cosmic hero team!**

REALLY?!

The "first" Guardians actually come from the future. Star-Lord and pals come face-to-face with the "originals" (Martinex, Vance Astro, Charlie-27 and Yondu) when they visit in the year 3009!

IDENTITY CRISIS?

The team almost name themselves "Rocket Raccoon and his Human Hangers-On" or "Groot and the Branches". Then they meet Vance Astro, formerly in a team named the "Guardians of the Galaxy", and "borrow" that name!

WHEN GOOD GUYS GO BAD!

HARD CHOICES

Magician Adam Warlock is a friend of the Guardians, but while attempting to heal a gap in space-time, his body is taken over by his evil side, the Magus! Magus uses an illusion to make several of the Guardians seem dead, so an angry Star-Lord takes down his old friend.

Gamora

The **Guardians of the Galaxy** are a **motley crew** of adventurers that travel across space, battling alien bad guys, confronting **cosmic threats** and **blowing things up.** Are they **heroes** or a gang of **troublemakers?** Maybe they're a little of both!

Rocket Raccoon

Groot

NEW RECRUIT
Tony Stark decides to take a holiday in space, but he is attacked by the alien Badoon. The Guardians come to Iron Man's rescue, and he ends up joining the team for a while.

DOUBLE TROUBLE

ROCKET & GROOT
Alien TV exec **Mojo** kidnaps **Rocket and Groot** and pits them against bizarre enemies as part of a **reality-TV show** on **Mojoworld**. The show is a hit, and Mojo makes **big money** selling Rocket and Groot **action figures!**

TOP 5
Guardians of the Galaxy

1 **STAR-LORD** (Peter Quill) – a roguish Earthling who can't help being a hero!

2 **ROCKET RACCOON** – a genetically engineered raccoon with plenty of weapons and even more attitude!

3 **DRAX THE DESTROYER** – a super-warrior created to take down Thanos.

4 **GROOT** – a treelike alien from Planet X, and Rocket's best bud!

5 **GAMORA** – the deadliest woman in the Galaxy! Trained by Thanos as an assassin, but soon sees the error of her ways.

BACK FROM THE DEAD!
Thanos plans to destroy the universe, and, when **Gamora** he tries to stop him, he kills her. **Adam Warlock** uses the Time Gem to project her spirit into a **new body!**

DADDY ISSUES
Star-Lord (Peter Quill) has a human mother, but his father J'son, alias **Jason of Spartax**, is the ruthless leader of the **Spartoi Empire!** He wants Peter to rule by his side, but Peter can't stand his dastardly dad!

JUST ADD WATER
Groot can regrow from just a **twig**, which is handy, as he tends to **get blown up a lot!** Rocket just collects a cutting and grows a **"new"** **Groot** in a pot.

Star-Lord

"NEVER doubt a raccoon."

FURRY ENCOUNTER
Rocket Raccoon first meets a Super Hero when he is stranded on the bizarre planet of **Halfworld** – with the Hulk! The two team up to take down the evil mole **Judson Jakes!**

REALLY?!

A **transporter glitch** sends the Defenders to a universe called **"Here",** where cute fuzzy animals **talk in rhyme.** To get back home, **Namor** straps on **ruby red slippers** and they all hold hands and say, "There's **no place** like the place I came from before I came **Here!"**

Namor

Luke Cage

FAST FACTS

FOUNDING MEMBERS: Dr Strange, Hulk, Namor, Silver Surfer

KEY MEMBERS: Luke Cage, Iron Fist, Red She-Hulk, Ant-Man (Scott Lang), Black Cat, Valkyrie, Nighthawk, Moondragon

FOES: Egghead's Emissaries of Evil, Satan, Yandroth, Headmen, Nul, Nebulon, Wrecking Crew

Red She-Hulk

Iron Fist

Doctor Strange

77
The number of past and present Defenders

FUTURE HEROES

In an alternate year 2510, **Earth is dying.** Reed and Sue Richards create a new team of **Defenders** and save all of the planet's six billion inhabitants – by sending them **back in time!**

TELL ME MORE!

The Defenders are formed when Doctor Strange enlists Namor the Sub-Mariner, the Hulk and the Silver Surfer to stop the evil Yandroth and his Omegatron from detonating every nuclear weapon on Earth.

LAST LINE OF DEFENCE

The Defenders are there when you need them – especially if you're facing a **magical threat!** Often led by **Doctor Strange,** this team of Super Heroes bands together out of necessity – when **defence** is the best form of **attack!**

BEST KNOWN FOR
COMING TOGETHER IN THE NICK OF TIME

ALTERNATE UNIVERSE

On (Earth-1610), the Defenders aren't that nice. The team have **no superpowers** and are far more interested in **fame** than being heroes. Desperate for power, they even **team up with Loki!**

AAARRGHH!!

SATAN pulls the Defenders **INTO HELL** where he forces them to face a series of **DIRE CHALLENGES.** If they fail, he will take over the Earth for **A THOUSAND YEARS!**

TOP 4
Defenders Lineups

1 **THE NEW DEFENDERS** – assembled by Beast; includes Angel, Valkyrie, Gargoyle, Iceman and Moondragon

2 **THE SECRET DEFENDERS** – to battle magical foes, Doctor Strange recruits the Hulk, Ghost Rider and the Silver Surfer

3 **THE LAST DEFENDERS** –Nighthawk, She-Hulk, Colossus and Blazing Skull protect New Jersey as part of the Fifty-State Initiative

4 **THE FEARLESS DEFENDERS** – an all-female team led by Misty Knight, Valkyrie and Dr Annabelle Riggs to face off against the villainous Caroline le Fay

HUSH-HUSH!

MI-13 is the British government's **first line of defence** against **super-powered** and **paranormal threats**. Overseen by secret agent **Pete Wisdom** and led by patriotic hero **Captain Britain**, MI-13 works behind the scenes to **keep the U.K. safe**!

> "Just you and me, children. Saving the world. From itself."

TOP 3
International Recruits

MI-13 is a British intelligence agency, but notable heroes from around the globe have joined its ranks.

1 BLADE – the legendary vampire hunter signs on when the agency clashes with Dracula and his vampire hordes. Hunts vampires along with Spitfire.

2 BLACK KNIGHT – former Avenger Dane Whitman, wielder of the Ebony Blade, joins to repel an alien invasion. In love with Faiza Hussain.

3 SHANG-CHI – Pete Wisdom calls on the Chinese Master of Kung Fu to defeat the Welsh Dragon, an ancient beast who finds a new calling as a crime lord.

S.H.I.E.L.D. DECLASSIFIED

JOINING THE DOTS
MI-13 is the latest British agency tasked with monitoring the unknown. Previous ones include S.T.R.I.K.E. (Special Tactical Reserve for International Key Emergencies), W.H.O. (Weird Happenings Organization), and Black Air.

Blade

Pete Wisdom

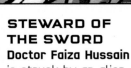

Faiza Hussain

STEWARD OF THE SWORD
Doctor Faiza Hussain is struck by an alien weapon and given near-complete control over biological organisms, allowing her to alter matter at a **subatomic** level. While serving with MI-13, she inherits **Excalibur**, the legendary sword of **King Arthur**!

TELL ME MORE!

Captain Britain's superhuman strength, speed, durability and flight are tied to his emotions. When he feels confident, he's nearly invincible. If he feels doubt, his powers weaken dramatically.

YESSS!!

DRACULA stages an invasion, believing the U.K's magical **ANTI-VAMPIRE** barriers have fallen. MI-13 has tricked the vampire lord, and most of his forces are **WIPED OUT** when they enter British airspace!

ALTERNATE UNIVERSE

The Captain Britain of **Earth-833** is a British version of **Spider-Man**!

OTHER NAMES: E.I.S. (Extraordinary Intelligence Service), "The Department"

LEADERS: Pete Wisdom, Captain Britain

TOP AGENTS: Alistaire Stewart (scientific advisor), Spitfire, Union Jack, Excalibur, Lionheart

BASES: Whitehall, The Shard (London, U.K.)

ALLIES: Meggan, Avengers, X-Men

FOES: Dracula, Mys-Tech, Oberon of Otherworld, Killpower, Plokta

Captain Britain

UPGRADED!

Lady Jacqueline Falsworth Crichton, alias **Spitfire**, is the daughter of the hero **Union Jack**. She was bitten by **Baron Blood** during World War II and turned into a **vampire** – but a good one! As well as vampire powers, she has **superhuman speed.**

Power Up!

HOT KNIVES! **PETE WISDOM** has the mutant ability to absorb heat and release it as **"HOT KNIVES"**. He can use his "hot knives" in various ways, such as **FIRING THEM** at opponents, using them as **CLAWS** or even creating a protective **FORCE FIELD.**

Q: Who is Captain Britain?

A: **Brian Braddock** is Earth's representative of the **Captain Britain Corps**, an **inter-dimensional league** of heroes granted powers by the magician **Merlin.** He is married to mutant empath **Meggan**, a Romany with **shape-shifting powers.**

Spitfire

TOP 5

Strangest MI-13 Agents

1
2
3
4
5

Black Knight

1,239

The speed that Captain Britain can fly in kilometres per hour (770 mph) – faster than the speed of sound.

COMPULSORY HELP

By order of the British prime minister, any Super Hero operating in the U.K. may be called on to assist MI-13 – whether they want to or not!

YESSS!! NICO and CHASE are kidnapped and forced to fight in wicked assassin Arcade's **BOOBY-TRAPPED** island arena. They survive and go undercover to infiltrate the Super Villain nation of **BAGALIA!**

VICTOR MANCHA

CHASE STEIN

BEST KNOWN FOR

PREVENTING THEIR MUMS AND DADS FROM TAKING OVER THE WORLD!

Power Up!

TIME FOR A SNOOZE
Molly Hayes, the youngest original Runaway, possesses immense **STRENGTH** and is nearly **INVULNERABLE.** However, using her powers makes her really **SLEEPY.** Even heroes need **NAPS!**

A BUMPY RIDE!
Chase pilots the group's **ship,** the **Leapfrog.** This frog-shaped vehicle – stolen from Chase's evil inventor parents – doesn't actually fly, it **jumps!**

RUNNING OUT OF TIME
The Runaways are **thrown back in time** to the year **1907** when a mission goes wrong! They get involved in a **super-powered turf war** and rescue young **plant-manipulating** mutant Klara Prast, who returns with them to the present.

Q: So what *is* the Pride?!

A: The Pride is a wealthy, powerful **gang of Super Villains,** formed of six couples. They are sworn to serve the **Gibborim** – a **race of giants** who want to **wipe out** humanity.

WHEN GOOD GUYS go **BAD!**

TREACHERY!
Alex Wilder, original leader of the Runaways, betrays the team to gain his evil parents' approval.

FUGITIVES!

What would **you** do if you found out your parents were secretly members of Super Villain clan, the **Pride?!?** If you were the **Runaways,** you'd steal a **magical staff,** a pair of **fire-shooting gauntlets** and a telepathically linked **dinosaur** – and **hit the road!**

S.H.I.E.L.D. DECLASSIFIED

LIKE FATHER, LIKE SON?
Victor Mancha is a cyborg, built by Ultron using cloned DNA and advanced nanotechnology. Ultron hopes to plant his "son" among the Avengers as a double agent, but Victor rejects his programming and becomes a true hero.

"Lots of kids think their parents are evil. Mine really were. Honestly."

UPGRADED!

The Leapfrog is **destroyed** when **missiles** tear apart the team's Malibu hideout. Luckily, Victor **salvages** the ship's computer and installs it in a new, upgraded Leapfrog that can **Fly**!

KLARA PRAST

NICO MINORU

FAST FACTS

KEY MEMBERS:
Nico, Chase, Gertrude, Karolina, Molly, Old Lace, Victor, Klara, Xavin

FRIENDS: Young Avengers, Avengers Academy, Cloak & Dagger

FOES: The Pride, Majesdanian Light Brigade, Arcade

BASE: Malibu, California (formerly beneath La Brea Tar Pits)

HANDLE WITH CARE!

Nico channels her magic through the **Staff of One**. This hugely powerful artefact has just two **drawbacks:**
1. Nico may only use a spell **once,** or the staff will backfire.
2. The staff **cannot** bring the dead back to life.

WHAT?!

Old Lace is a **genetically engineered dinosaur** from the **87th century** who shares a **telepathic bond** with Gertrude! ▶

IDENTITY CRISIS?

Karolina Dean is raised as a human, but one day she discovers that both she and her parents are secretly solar-powered aliens from another world, Majesdane!

MOLLY HAYES

SQUABBLES & SUPERPOWERS

Think your siblings are **annoying?** Try dealing with a little brother who can turn into a **cloud** – or a baby sister able to **disintegrate matter!** When they aren't fighting crime, the young heroes of **Power Pack** are usually **fighting one another!**

TELL ME MORE!

Horse-headed Kymellian scientist Aelfyre Whitemane is wounded by alien Snarks while defending physicist Dr Power's new invention. Before Whitemane dies, he bestows his powers onto Dr Power's children, along with his spaceship!

UPGRADED!

The team's powers often **swap around,** so they find new ways to use their gifts. Jack works out how to use Alex's powers to throw a gravity-powered "Super-G" punch.

Alex Power is a teen **genius,** so Reed Richards drafts him into the **Future Foundation,** made up of the most **brilliant young minds** on the planet.

JULIE

ALEX

FAST FACTS

ABILITIES:
Gravity control – Alex (Gee) • Energy absorption/disintegration –Katie (Energizer) • **Density manipulation** – Jack (Mass Master) • **High-speed flight** – Julie (Lightspeed)

NOT-SO-FRIENDLY FOES:
Snarks, Kurse, Bogeyman

PARENTS: Dr James Power, Margaret Power

IDENTITY CRISIS!

"Let's see... you got my power and I got Jack's power and Jack got Alex's power and Alex got your power! What a mess!" —Julie

"I'll take a crazy villain over a mad little sister any day..."
JACK

JACK

KATIE

Power Up!

SOAR
Julie takes a while to master her flying abilities. At first, she can only stay aloft while **ACCELERATING** – and slow down by running **INTO** something!

SHAPE-SHIFT
Boisterous Jack can transform into a **GAS**, or become solid and drop onto enemies as a "**JACK HAMMER**".

REALLY?!
"Snark" is just a nickname for the evil alien **Z'nrx** race, as their real name is **unpronounceable** by human tongues!

FAMILY CONNECTIONS
Space vessel **Smartship Friday** is the Power Pack's main mode of transport. The **computer A.I.** that runs the ship is genderless, but the kids think of Friday as a **surrogate space mother**.

Top 4 Goofiest Codenames
1. Mistress of Density – Julie
2. Molecula – Julie
3. Counterweight – Katie
4. Powerpax – Alex

Power Up!

CRUMBLE
Katie is just **FIVE** when she obtains her disintegration powers. When Norse monster Kurse attacks, she **TOPPLES** a building onto him – and then **FEELS BAD** about it!

MANIPULATE
Alex's control over gravity lets him make objects **WEIGHTLESS**, or increase the **PRESSURE** on bad guys. He can even **FLY** with homemade wings!

QUEST FOR REVENGE!
Dr Power's greedy ex-boss, **Douglas Carmody**, blames Power Pack for his **financial ruin**. His vengeful **obsession** leads him to Limbo, where he is transformed into the **grotesque Bogeyman**!

WHAT?!

Physicist Dr Walter Langkowski accidentally opens a **portal** to the magical **Realm of Great Beasts**, allowing the monster **Tanaraq** to possess him. Now Walter can transform into the massively strong and hairy **Sasquatch**!

Shaman

Sasquatch

Aurora

Guardian

FAMILY CONNECTIONS

Originally, twins **Northstar and Aurora** could only access their full powers when they were in **direct contact.** Now, both mutant heroes can independently summon massive bursts of **devastating light,** which can take the form of **concussive blasts!**

FROM THE SEA

Marrina is a member of the highly adaptive **Plodex alien race.** Marrina's egg pod lands in the ocean and she later acquires **unique amphibious abilities** – which she puts to use as Alpha Flight's most **hotheaded team member!**

Snowbird

Northstar

Marrina

TELL ME MORE!

As Alpha Flight's former leader, Guardian (inventor James "Mac" Hudson) wears a suit that gives him flight, body armour and the ability to fire powerful bursts of energy.

Puck

DEPT. H DECLASSIFIED

FROM GAMMA TO ALPHA

Overseen by Department H, Alpha Flight isn't known as "Canada's Premier Super Team" for nothing! The department trains would-be heroes as Gamma Flight. When they're ready, they take to the field as Beta Flight. Only the best of the best graduate to Alpha Flight status!

INTO ORBIT
Based on a space station, **Alpha Flight (Space Program)** gets a new commander – **Carol Danvers**, alias **Captain Marvel!** Dealing with threats to the galaxy, the elite team comprises **Puck**, **Aurora**, **Sasquatch** and science officer **Wendy Kawasaki**.

CANADA'S CHAMPIONS

Whenever **Canada** is threatened by **mythical marauders** or **super-powered menaces**, the government doesn't make an international call to **Avengers Tower.** It contacts its very own Super Hero team – **Alpha Flight!**

HANDLE WITH CARE!
First Nations member Dr Michael Twoyoungmen, also known as **Shaman**, can draw all sorts of **potions** and **artefacts** from his **enchanted medicine bag**. It takes years of training just to **look in it!**

BACK FROM THE DEAD!
When Guardian **seemingly dies,** an alien, fishlike race named the **Qwrlln** fuse his Guardian suit to his body. The result? They turn him into a **cyborg**, but they save his life!

ANIMAL MAGIC
Power Up!
SNOWBIRD is the half-human daughter of the Inuit goddess **NELVANNA**. She can transform into an albino version of any northern animal, such as a **SHARP-EYED OWL** – or a **SHARP-CLAWED POLAR BEAR!**

3m (10ft)
1.1m (3ft 6in)

Alpha Flight members come in all shapes and sizes, from the **diminutive Puck** to the **towering Sasquatch!**

LOOKS AREN'T EVERYTHING!

The Avengers **fly high** above sunny streets, but other champions **lurk deep underground**. The **Legion of Monsters** are **shunned** for their horrific appearance, but they **protect** their fellow creatures of the night from **monster hunters** and **hateful humans!**

The curse of **lycanthropy** has blighted generations of Jacob "Jack" Russell's family. Jack usually keeps his **werewolf side** under control, but sometimes he gives into his rage. The result? Clashes with **Moon Knight** and **Dr Strange!**

WHEN BAD GUYS

CLUED UP
Satana is drafted into Luke Cage's **Thunderbolts** to **beef up** the team's magical defences. Her first-hand knowledge of **demons** comes in handy when the Asgardian, Kuurth, possesses the body of fellow team member Juggernaut!

YEGCH!

The Legion of Monsters guards **Monster Metropolis**, located deep below New York City in the filthy, smelly sewers! It's a safe haven for others of their kind.

UPGRADED!

3,000 years ago, warrior N'Kantu was **magically embalmed** by an evil priest and kept in a tomb for millennia – **awake, but paralysed!** Now he's free, the **mystical fluids** that flow in him grant amazing strength.

FAMILY CONNECTIONS
Satana isn't known as the **Devil's Daughter** for nothing: She inherits vastly powerful **dark magicks** from her demonic father – making her one of the most powerful **witches** on Earth.

WEREWOLF BY NIGHT

AAAARRGHH!!!
N'Kantu is imprisoned during the superhuman civil war. How? Iron Man designs a **CAGE** of **ROARING FLAMES** to contain the mystical mummy!

TELL ME MORE!
Man-Thing guards the Nexus of All Realities – a gateway between different dimensions – through which he can teleport himself and his teammates.

REALLY?!
Frank Castle, the **Punisher**, is **chopped** to **pieces** by the assassin Daken. Morbius **stitches** him back together into a patchwork "FrankenCastle!"

MAN-THING

"I'm the primary caregiver to all manner of creepy crawlies."

MORBIUS

Legendary **monster hunter Elsa Bloodstone** is actually an **ally** of the Legion and the peaceful inhabitants of Monster Metropolis: These beasts **police themselves** and pose **little threat** to humans!

ELSA BLOODSTONE

One of **Peter Parker's** Horizon Labs colleagues works behind closed doors in a **protective suit**. Peter discovers it's none other than **Dr Michael Morbius** – searching for a **cure** for his vampirism!

WHAT ARE YOU LOOKING AT?

WIDE, WEBBED FACE GILLS – allow Manphibian to breathe underwater.

SHARP CLAWS – for attacking and defending.

TOUGH, ARMOUR-LIKE SKIN – can even withstand missile attacks!

FAST FACTS

MEMBERS:
Werewolf by Night, Man-Thing, Morbius the Living Vampire, Satana, N'Kantu the Living Mummy, Manphibian

BASE: Monster Metropolis

ALLIES: Punisher, Elsa Bloodstone, Ghost Rider

FOES: Hunter of Monster Special Forces, Robert Hellsgaard

Q: What's a "Living Vampire"?

A: **Unlike** most bloodsuckers, Morbius's need for blood stems from a scientific **accident**, not a supernatural curse. He's vulnerable to sunlight but is **not truly undead**, and he's **immune** to holy water, garlic and crucifixes.

MANPHIBIAN

"Thisss is jussst how we look."

WHAT?!

To gain **knowledge of the future**, Odin tears out his own eye and throws it into the **Well of Wisdom**. The eye grows and takes on **a life of its own**, travelling the universe and giving enigmatic advice to Thor.

TOP 5

No-Good Gods

1 **AMATSU-MIKABOSHI** – Japanese God of Evil; kills Zeus and launches the Chaos War to wipe out all of existence

2 **LOKI** – Asgardian God of Mischief obsessed with power and getting one over on his brother Thor

3 **SETH** – Egyptian God of the Dead; imprisons other Egyptian gods and inspires Apocalypse to conquer the world

4 **PLUTO** – Greek God of Death; plots to conquer Olympus and the world, but is defeated by Earth's Super Heroes

5 **HELA** – Queen of the Dead; wants to bring all mortals and the gods of Asgard into Hel

HANDLE WITH CARE!

Odin has a powerful weapon – **Gungnir, the Spear of Heaven!** It's made of Uru metal and can **channel the Odinforce**. Unlike Thor's hammer, Mjolnir, you don't have to be worthy to wield it.

Q: Why do the gods of Earth no longer interact with mortals?

A: 1,000 years ago the **Celestials** made them promise **not to interfere** with humanity! That's why Zeus and Odin get so angry when Hercules and Thor keep going to Earth and **playing the hero!**

GODS AMONG US

YESSS!! To protect Earth, Odin builds a **MIGHTY WEAPON**: a massive suit of armour named the **DESTROYER**. It contains the life-forces of **EVERY ASGARDIAN!**

REALLY?!

Even gods fear **Atum the God Eater,** also known as the Demogorge. He **lives in the sun** and devours deities that turn against humanity. He suffers a **fatal case of indigestion** when he swallows the Skrull god Sl'gur't!

TELL ME MORE!

The Asgardians and Olympians get most of the attention thanks to Thor and Hercules, but Earth is home to many families of gods. They include the Gods of Heliopolis (Egyptian), the Vodu (African), the Amatsu-Kami (Japanese), the Xian (Chinese) and the Manidoog (Native American). The gods of Earth meet at the Council of Godheads to decide matters of heavenly importance.

WOW!

7,620

The height in metres (25,000ft) of the massive Godkiller armour, built by the Aspirants to kill the Celestials.

TEAM PLAYER

When the Skrulls launch their **Secret Invasion**, Hercules leads a **God Squad** to defend Earth. It includes Amadeus Cho, Atum, Snowbird, Ajak of the Eternals and Amatsu-Mikaboshi. Amatsu **betrays Herc** and unleashes the devastating **Chaos War!**

The Multiverse is home to **many gods.** They usually **stay out** of mortal affairs – but when they do get involved, the results can be **Earth-shattering!**

S.H.I.E.L.D.

FAST FACTS

FULL NAME:
Strategic Hazard Intervention, Espionage, and Logistics Directorate

ORIGIN: Founded by the U.S. government with the help of Tony Stark

HEADQUARTERS: S.H.I.E.L.D. Helicarrier

ABILITIES: Advanced weaponry, technology, surveillance, intelligence, massive manpower

ALLIES: Avengers, S.W.O.R.D., Secret Avengers

FOES: Hydra, A.I.M., Masters of Evil

S.H.I.E.L.D. DECLASSIFIED

THE HELICARRIER
S.H.I.E.L.D.'s primary vehicle and HQ is a flying aircraft carrier designed by Tony Stark and built by Stark Industries. There have been several versions – and a number of spectacular crashes!

S.H.I.E.L.D. DECLASSIFIED

S.H.I.E.L.D.'S FLYING CARS
Stark Industries manufactures a wide range of flying cars for S.H.I.E.L.D. These armoured sports cars not only fly at high speeds and altitudes, they can also travel underwater as submarines.

NUMBER CRUNCH!

3000
Active S.H.I.E.L.D. agents prior to the superhuman civil war

885km (550 miles)
Maximum distance flown by a S.H.I.E.L.D. flying car

10 hours
Maximum oxygen supply inside a flying car

Mach 2.1
Quinjet max speed

S.H.I.E.L.D. DECLASSIFIED

ROBOT REPLACEMENTS
Life Model Decoys (LMDs) are androids developed by S.H.I.E.L.D. to impersonate people. Externally, these robots are indistinguishable from living humans. They are controlled remotely and have superhuman strength.

S.H.I.E.L.D. DECLASSIFIED

THE QUINJET
Quinjets are originally created by Black Panther's Wakanda Design Group. They are often stowed aboard S.H.I.E.L.D. Helicarriers, ready to transport agents for dangerous missions – even in space! Quinjets are capable of vertical take-off and landings.

UPGRADED!

Tony Stark wins the superhuman civil war and becomes director of S.H.I.E.L.D. after Maria Hill resigns. He designs a new red-and-gold Helicarrier, makes improvements and raises morale.

TOP 4
Directors of S.H.I.E.L.D.

1 **RICK STONER** – the first director; assassinated by Hydra terrorists

2 **NICK FURY, SR.** – ageless director for 40 years; still active in team

3 **TONY STARK (IRON MAN)** – director after the superhuman civil war; sacked for failing to anticipate Skrull invasion

4 **MARIA HILL** – the strongest leader since Nick Fury; has had more than one spell as director

NOOOOO!! Nick Fury has an **AUTONOMOUS** Life Model Decoy known as Max Fury. It becomes **SO DANGEROUS** that Nick tries to destroy it – but the LMD **GETS AWAY!**

WHEN BAD GUYS GO GOOD!

DARK REIGN
Norman Osborn replaces Tony Stark (Iron Man) as director of S.H.I.E.L.D. after Stark fails to prevent the Skrulls' Secret Invasion. Osborn renames the organisation H.A.M.M.E.R.

WORLD SAVED!

S.H.I.E.L.D. is Earth's **front line** of defence, combating **global threats** from Super Villains, supernatural menaces, alien invaders and terrorist groups. **S.H.I.E.L.D.** is equipped with **cutting-edge technology** and commands a force of **superbly trained agents.**

FAST AND FURIOUS!

They are **father and son.** They share the name **Nick Fury** and a **common cause:** safeguarding the U.S.A. – and the world – from **all manner** of threats as the **main men of S.H.I.E.L.D.!**

FAST FACTS

FULL NAME: Nicholas Joseph Fury

STRENGTHS: Expert strategist, vast combat experience, fast healing

WEAKNESSES: Blind in left eye, disregard for rules and ethics

ALLIES: Dum Dum Dugan, Daisy Johnson, Spider-Man, Avengers, S.H.I.E.L.D., Secret Warriors, Howling Commandos

FOES: Axis, Red Skull, Hydra, Doctor Doom, Taskmaster

BEST KNOWN FOR

BEING A RUTHLESS S.H.I.E.L.D. DIRECTOR

Q: Who are the Howling Commandos?

A: They are a bunch of misfit but brave World War II soldiers. **Sergeant Nick Fury** leads them against Axis villains such as **Red Skull** and **Baron von Strucker**.

Nick Fury launches an investigation to discover who murdered Uatu the Watcher and stole one of his **all-seeing eyes.** He omits to mention that **he did it himself!**

"Nick Fury ain't watchin' the end o' the *WORLD* in bed, Mister!"

FULL NAME: Nicholas Joseph Fury (formerly Marcus Johnson)

STRENGTHS: Expert combatant, infinity formula in blood gives even greater healing and anti-aging powers than Nick Sr.

WEAKNESSES: Blind in left eye

ALLIES: Avengers, Secret Avengers, Phillip Coulson, Wolverine, Nick Fury Sr., S.H.I.E.L.D., U.S. Army Rangers

FOES: Orion, Taskmaster, Leviathan

BEST KNOWN FOR

BEING NOT QUITE AS RUTHLESS AS HIS DAD

Q: How does Nick Fury Jr. lose his eye?

A: Fury Sr.'s enemy **Orion** wants to extract **the Infinity Formula** in the veins of Fury's son. Father and son stop Orion, but the villain takes Nick Jr.'s eye – a **spiteful act** to make him look **more like his father.**

TOP 6

Howling Commandos

1 **DUM DUM DUGAN** – circus strongman

2 **IZZY COHEN** – car mechanic

3 **GABE JONES** – jazz trumpeter

4 **JONATHAN JUNIPER** – eager beaver, Ivy League college graduate

5 **DINO MANELLI** – dashing actor with matinee idol looks

6 **REBEL RALSTON** – skilled horseback rider

SCORPIO

FAMILY DISCONNECTIONS

Nick Jr. follows in his father's footsteps, but not all the Furys are on the same side. Fury Sr.'s brother, Jake, becomes the **villain Scorpio** and joins Hydra. Nick Jr.'s brother, Mikal, **tries to kill his father!**

TELL ME MORE!

Fury (Sr.) tricks a team of heroes into joining him on an **illegal mission** to overthrow villainous Latvarian prime minister, Lucia von Bardas. When it's over he **wipes the team's memories!**

AAARRGHH!!

Fury's dark deeds are **PUNISHED** when the Watchers force him to take dead Uatu's place, **HELPLESSLY** watching events on Earth as **"THE UNSEEN".**

ALTERNATE UNIVERSE

On Earth-1610, Nick Fury is a test subject in **Project Rebirth**, and given an **super-strength** injection. He loses his eye in the Gulf War. As S.H.I.E.L.D. director, he forms an Avengers taskforce called "the Ultimates".

BETWEEN...

The first issue of *Sgt. Fury and His Howling Commandos* appeared in May 1963. Stan Lee and Jack Kirby were confident of success despite the comic book's rather unwieldy title.

...THE PANELS

SPY SOLDIERS

S.H.I.E.L.D. agents undergo rigorous **spy school training,** learning fighting techniques, how to use the latest technology and much more. Most operatives are **unswervingly loyal** – and some even carry on serving **after they're dead!**

CONFIDENTIAL

AGENTS OF S.H.I.E.L.D.

If you should ever penetrate S.H.I.E.L.D. security (unlikely!), here are some faces you may meet…

- **NICK FURY JR.** – the secret son of C.I.A. agent Nia Jones and Nick Fury Sr. Heads up the Secret Avengers Initiative with Phil Coulson.

- **DEATHLOK** (Henry Hayes) – every covert team should have it's own cyborg assassin!

CONFIDENTIAL

- **MELINDA MAY** (Cavalry) – one of S.H.I.E.L.D.'s top agents with amazing fighting skills

- **JEMMA SIMMONS** – may only have a short time to live after being infected by an A.I.M. DNA bomb!

- **LEO FITZ** – British agent who has been on dangerous missions involving magic and demons

- **DUM DUM DUGAN** –served alongside Nick Fury in World War II. One of S.H.I.E.L.D.'s first agents, now a Life Model Decoy robot!

CONFIDENTIAL

- **MOCKINGBIRD** – Barbara "Bobbi" Morse (Agent 19), a baton-wielding bio-chemist and high- level agent. Has also served with the West Coast Avengers.

- **QUAKE** (Daisy Johnson) – can create seismic disturbances with her hands. Causes such a shake-up in Nick Fury Sr.'s Secret Warriors team that she briefly ends up as director of S.H.I.E.L.D.

- **AGENT 13** (Sharon Carter) – Peggy Carter's niece, and longtime girlfriend of Steve Rogers. The first leader of Femme Force, a team of female agents.

- **PHIL "CHEESE" COULSON** – a high-ranking member, often helming his own elite Secret Avengers team, sometimes with best friend Nick Fury Jr. Phil is a big Super Hero fan!

> ## "I'm a guy with a *PLAN.*"
> PHIL COULSON

WHEN GOOD GIRLS GO BAD!

MADAME HYDRA
The Contessa Valentina Allegra de Fontaine is a loyal S.H.I.E.L.D. agent and Nick Fury's love interest for decades. Then she joins terror group Hydra as the ruthless Madame Hydra!

REALLY?!

Mechanical menace M.O.D.O.K. has a secret agenda when he teams up with S.H.I.E.L.D. He plans to **kill** Director Maria Hill, but ends up **crying tears** of love!

LOVE PUNCH

The first time Nick Fury meets the Contessa he totally underestimates her combat skills. His embarrassment soon turns to love!

S.H.I.E.L.D. DECLASSIFIED

THE GIFT OF ETERNAL LIFE
The amazing robot technology showcased in Life Model Decoys dates back to Leonardo da Vinci's time! Some LMDs are so advanced that a human consciousness can be uploaded into them. This enables a person to, in effect, live on forever!

NOOOOOO!!

Even after **DEATH**, Dum Dum Dugan carries on working for S.H.I.E.L.D. – as a **LIFE MODEL DECOY.** Dugan doesn't know he's a **ROBOT** – and is dismayed when he finds out!

BACK FROM THE DEAD!

Top agent Jasper Sitwell is **shot dead** by a brainwashed **Black Widow.** He returns as a **zombie** and joins S.H.I.E.L.D.'s Howling Commandos!

159

S.H.I.E.L.D. OPERATIONS

Battling **terror groups,** facing down **Super Villains** and dealing with **sneaky extraterrestrial invasions** is no easy task. Throw in sudden outbreaks of **treachery** and **betrayal** from within and it's a wonder that **S.H.I.E.L.D.** is still going strong!

TOP 6
Most Wanted Foes

1 **BARON VON STRUCKER** – death-dealing terrorist leader!

2 **RED SKULL** – death-dealing terrorist leader!

3 **BARON ZEMO** – death-dealing terrorist leader and scientist!

4 **MADAME HYDRA** – death-dealing terrorist leader!

5 **ARNIM ZOLA** – death-dealing scientist!

6 **SCORPIO** – death-dealing terrorist!

S.H.I.E.L.D. DECLASSIFIED

SECRET WARRIORS
When Nick Fury Sr. (former Director of S.H.I.E.L.D.) uncovers a secret invasion of Skrulls, he knows nowhere is safe. He assembles the Secret Warriors – a young, super-secret squad, some of whom have super-powered parents.

REALLY?!

If a mission is **too strange** even for S.H.I.E.L.D., they send in the **Howling Commandos** – led by a Life Model Decoy (LMD) of **Dum Dum Dugan**, with the help of **Man-Thing, Hit Monkey, Vampire by Night, Teen Abomination, Warwolf** and more. From Plant Zombies and dark magic to the **strangest monstrosities,** these guys have it covered!

AAARRGHH!!!
Iron Man's shortlived role as **DIRECTOR** of S.H.I.E.L.D. ends when his armour goes **BERSERK** with an alien **COMPUTER VIRUS.** He ends up being **FIRED** by the **U.S. PRESIDENT** himself!

TELL ME MORE!

Artist Leonardo Da Vinci, physicist Isaac Newton and astronomer Galileo Galilei were once members of the Brotherhood of the Shield! Long before the days of Nick Fury or the Avengers, these heroes were the first to defeat Galactus, the Brood and the Celestials.

YESSS!! Former agent **MENTALLO** tries to conquer S.H.I.E.L.D. and control Nick Fury's mind. Luckily, Fury is able to **TIP OFF** the S.H.I.E.L.D. ESP team, cueing Tony Stark to neutralize an **H-BOMB** – and win the day!

TEAM PLAYER

Captain America is a key **player** in many S.H.I.E.L.D. operations. His **link** with Nick Fury dates back to **World War II**. Cap has also had a **close relationship** with high-ranking operative **Sharon Carter**.

"Our **TARGET** is in possession of the Cosmic Cube. So surprise is **VITAL.**"

DASTARDLY DEED!

Hydra has been trying to **topple** S.H.I.E.L.D. since World War II. Hydra's science division, Advanced Idea Mechanics, **infiltrates** S.H.I.E.L.D. with **LMDs**, and also tries to ruin Mr Fantastic's **wedding** with a **Vortex bomb!**

ALTERNATE UNIVERSE

On planet Battleworld, the **Shield** is a **fortified, giant wall** that stands between Battleworld's **inhabitants** and a mixture of **zombies, Ultron's hordes** and villainous **monsters!**

SUPER VILLAIN TEAMS

MANY-HEADED MENACE

Cut off a head, and two more shall take its place! Named for the monster of Greek Myth, **Hydra** is the **most dangerous** and widespread **villainous organisation** on Earth. This **team of terror** spreads **corruption and violence** in a bid for **global domination!**

"HAIL HYDRA!"

FAILURE IS NOT AN OPTION!
Hydra does not accept **failure!** Unsuccessful agents are **executed** – or forced to fight for their lives in **duels to the death!**

S.H.I.E.L.D. DECLASSIFIED

ORIGINS UNKNOWN
The roots of Hydra may lie in ancient Egypt or medieval Japan, but the modern organisation was established by Nazi fanatic Baron von Strucker after World War II.

YESSS!!
Hydra unleashes a vast vehicle called the **TERROR-CARRIER** (similar to S.H.I.E.L.D.'s Helicarrier) to capture the **U.S. PRESIDENT**. A giant Yellowjacket (Hank Pym) rides it to destruction!

WHAT?!
After years of planning, **Hydra agents** infiltrate S.H.I.E.L.D. and **take it over!** **Baron von Strucker** believes he has defeated his old enemies, but then S.H.I.E.L.D. chief **Nick Fury** reveals that he's been **controlling Hydra** all along!

HANDLE WITH CARE!
Hydra's **Death Spore bomb** is set to wipe out **everyone on Earth** – except the Hydra agents in Baron von Strucker's island base! **Nick Fury** has other ideas and blows up von Strucker and his HQ instead!

BACK FROM THE DEAD!
Baron von Strucker is killed on **Hydra Island**, but his faithful agents find the Baron's remains – and **sacrifice** themselves to return him to life!

BACK FROM THE DEAD!

When Hydra leader **Viper** is shot dead, she is brought back to life by a horrible Hydra labs creation – **Hive parasites**. As a result, she looks like a **humanoid octopus!**

Baron von Strucker

Power Up!

SATAN CLAW

This mechanical glove unleashes **ELECTRIC SHOCKS** and gives Baron von Strucker enhanced **STRENGTH** – so that he can battle Nick Fury toe to toe! It's been upgraded with a **GATLING GUN**, a **TELEPORTER** and a **NUCLEAR REACTOR!**

TOP 3

Hydra Splinter Groups

THESE GROUPS WERE ONCE PART OF HYDRA—BUT ARE NOW ITS ENEMIES!

1 **A.I.M.** – Advanced Idea Mechanics is Hydra's hi-tech research branch, until it goes independent after Baron von Strucker is killed on Hydra Island.

2 **SECRET EMPIRE** – Hydra creates the Secret Empire to cause trouble and draw attention away from Hydra itself. It specialises in political corruption and destroying heroes' reputations!

3 **THE HAND** – this clan of evil ninja helped to found the modern Hydra, but it has also fiercely opposed it at times.

BETWEEN...

Movies, books and TV series about spies were all the rage in 1965, so Marvel's Stan Lee and Jack Kirby introduced Hydra in *Strange Tales* #135 as the evil equivalent of S.H.I.E.L.D.

...THE PANELS

UNDERCOVER

Jake Fury steals the **identity** of **Kraken** – one of Hydra's most **ruthless assassins** – and helps his long-lost brother Nick start a **civil war** within Hydra, and **kill** Baron von Strucker!

AAARRGHH!! The mysterious **SHADOW COUNCIL** sets up its own nation of **BAGALIA**. Don't go there – a Masters of Evil team made up of **HUNDREDS** of members serves as the **POLICE FORCE!**

Moonstone

Goliath

TROUBLEMAKERS!

ALTERNATE UNIVERSE

In the **Heroes Reborn** universe, **Black Knight** has grand plans to reshape the world with his Masters of Evil. Unfortunately, one of Dr Doom's **Doombots** blows his head off, before **eliminating** all but one of the Masters!

Wrecker

Q: How was the first Masters of Evil team created?

A: **Baron Heinrich Zemo** discovers that his supposedly dead foe, Captain America, is alive and a member of the **Avengers** – so he forms the **Masters of Evil** to **destroy** them all! Zemo **handpicks** each Super Villain member to match the powers of each Avenger.

The first **Masters of Evil** was founded by a mad scientist, but **many other teams** have since taken the name. They all have three things in common: loads of **B-list bad guys, wacky plans** to defeat Super Heroes and a love for **wreaking havoc!**

Mister Hyde

REALLY?!

On their first mission, **Heinrich Zemo's** Masters of Evil stop the Avengers in their tracks by spraying them with **super-sticky Adhesive X glue.** Luckily, Earth's Mightiest Heroes use a cylinder of **Super-Dissolver** to melt the glue and **break free!**

HANDLE WITH CARE!

Egghead and his Masters of Evil kidnap **Hank Pym** to help Egghead build a **longevity machine.** Instead, Hank builds a weapons system with **force fields, cadmium tentacles** and a **disruption stunner** to take down the Masters **single-handed!**

Bulldozer

Thunderball

Titania

Piledriver

WHEN GOOD GUYS GO BAD!

TRIPLE BLUFF!
The mysterious Crimson Cowl assembles a new Masters of Evil team. The Avengers get a shock when they discover that the Cowl is none other than their beloved butler, Jarvis! Or is he...?!

Yellowjacket

Tiger Shark

DASTARDLY DEED!

Baron Helmut Zemo decides that the **best way** to beat the Avengers is by **swamping them with enemies!** He recruits an **18-strong** Masters of Evil team including Goliath and Bulldozer, which trashes **Avengers Mansion** – and the Avengers!

Absorbing Man

Helmut Zemo

WHEN BAD GUYS GO GOOD!

NOT WHAT HE EXPECTED
Baron Helmut Zemo has a cunning plan: His second Masters of Evil lineup pretends to be a team of heroes, the Thunderbolts! Zemo is thwarted when all the villains – except for him – decide that they like being liked and become heroes for real!

FAST FACTS

TEAM LEADERS:
Baron Helmut Zemo, Shadow Council, Ultron 5 (as Crimson Cowl), Egghead, Baron Heinrich Zemo, Doctor Octopus, Black Knight, Lightmaster

LAIR: Inaccessible (underground or mountaintops)

MAIN FOES: Avengers, Guardians of the Galaxy

CLAIM TO FAME: Capturing Avengers Mansion

FEELING SINISTER?

Just one thing unites **the Sinister Six**: They all **hate Spider-Man!** Six against one may not seem like a fair fight, but these bad guys spend as much time **fighting each other** as they do battling Spidey!

TELL ME MORE!

The first Sinister Six – Doc Ock, Kraven, Electro, Mysterio, Vulture and Sandman – all want a solo victory over Spider-Man. They attack him one at a time, but Spidey easily knocks them out!

AAARGHH!!

The **FUTURE FOUNDATION** explores a Caribbean island and is attacked by **ZOMBIE PIRATES!** However, the zombies turn out to be fakes – controlled by an **ALL-NEW SINISTER SIX.**

Just in case the untrustworthy Sandman betrays the team, Doc Ock always keeps a **melter-ray** handy – to heat him into solid glass.

Sandman

Doctor Octopus

REALLY?!

When Doctor Octopus **holds the world ransom,** Spider-Man tracks him down and is forced to battle **a new Sinister Six team** – made up of mind-controlled Avengers!

Vulture, Mysterio, Hobgoblin and Electro create a **"Sinister Five"** to get revenge on Doc Ock. To make Sandman join, they bomb the home of a family he's staying with – and blame Doc Ock!

DOUBLE TROUBLE!
The Green Goblin blackmails Spider-Man into busting him out of jail, then sends a double-size team, the Sinister Twelve, to squash the wall-crawler.

66

Alien TV boss Mojo assembles the "Sinister Sixty-Six" to fight Spider-Man.

Chameleon

Rhino

CRIME ON THE WING

Vulture (Adrian Toomes) is a founding member of the Sinister Six and one of Spidey's oldest enemies. His electromagnetic flying harness is great for aerial attacks and smash and grab raids!

Power Up!

TECH SUPPORT

The Sinister Six needs more firepower, so they take an **INTER-DIMENSIONAL TRIP** to steal hi-tech weapons! Armed with a new **FUTURISTIC ARSENAL**, the Six quickly knock Spidey out of action!

Mysterio

Electro

TOP **4**

Worst Teammates

1 **DOCTOR OCTOPUS** – mean and manipulative, Doc Ock blackmails, betrays and even mind-controls to get his way

2 **SANDMAN** – not such a bad guy, which is why he switches sides and fights for the good guys more than once

3 **MYSTERIO** –Spidey persuades him to sell out his boss when Doc Ock threatens to roast the world

4 **CHAMELEON** – this master of disguise can fool almost anyone – even other villains

The Sinister Six don't always **lose**! In one battle, they manage to beat up both Spidey and the **Incredible Hulk!**

ALTERNATE UNIVERSE

On **Earth-803**, New York is terrorized by techno-freaks known as the **Six Men of Sinestry.** Fortunately, they are **no match** for the costumed heroine **Lady Spider.**

LOOK OUT!

Criminal thug Aleksei Sytsevich permanently bonded to a super-tough exoskeleton. He becomes an enforcer for the Super Villains as the rampaging Rhino!

169

ARGUING AMONG THEMSELVES AND BEING DEFEATED

FAST FACTS

NAME: Lethal Legion

LEADERS: Grim Reaper, Count Nefaria

KEY MEMBERS: Living Laser, Man-Ape, Swordsman, Whirlwind, Black Talon

OBJECTIVE: Destroy the Avengers by any means possible!

HANDLE WITH CARE!

Grim Reaper has a **high-tech scythe** instead of a right hand. The scythe has a built-in knockout ray, electroshock circuit and energy blaster. It can also **spin** like a **buzzsaw**, become a **shield** and rotate **fast enough** for him **to fly!**

GOOD DAY

The Lethal Legion **almost defeat** the Avengers at the **first attempt!** They trap half the Avengers in a **giant hourglass** filled with poison gas – until the Vision **tricks Grim Reaper** into **breaking the glass!**

TOP 6
Not-So-Lethal Legionnaires

SWORDSMAN – handy with a sword, but not much else

MAN-APE – stronger than a gorilla, but dumb

TRAPSTER – great at squirting superglue!

PORCUPINE – invents a spiny suit with lasers, but sells it to avoid arrest

BATROC – acrobat with a great moustache, but looks alone can't defeat heroes!

WHIRLWIND – can spin like a deadly whirlwind, but only in a straight line

WHEN BAD GUYS GO GOOD!

BROTHERS IN BADNESS!
When Norman Osborn becomes Director of S.H.I.E.L.D. and renames it H.A.M.M.E.R., Grim Reaper recruits a new Lethal Legion – and gets his brother Wonder Man to join! For once, the Williams brothers are fighting on the same side!

YESSS!!

Not all the Lethal Legion's missions are **DISASTERS**. With help from **ULTRON** they storm the West Coast Avengers' base, free teammate Goliath, then **KIDNAP WONDER MAN** and **HANK PYM!**

BAD DAY

Crime boss **Count Nefaria** gives the Living Laser, Power Man (Erik Josten), and Whirlwind a job in a **new Lethal Legion** team. He offers to **boost their powers**, then betrays them. The shifty Count **steals their powers** so he can take on **the Avengers!**

LETHAL LOSERS

The **Lethal Legion** aren't the greatest villains. Their founder, **Grim Reaper,** wants a Super Villain team to **take down** Earth's Mightiest Heroes, but just **can't find the right teammates!**

BACK FROM THE DEAD!

Vampiric mutant Nekra loves the Grim Reaper. When he dies she brings him back to life – **as a zombie!** To stay living, he is forced to absorb one life every 24 hours – and he starts with **Nekra!**

TELL ME MORE!

Grim Reaper starts the Lethal Legion because he blames the Avengers for the apparent death of his brother, Wonder Man. However, his loyalties become confused when he finds out that Wonder Man's brain patterns were used to program Vision!

FAMILY CONNECTIONS

Lethal Legion boss **Grim Reaper** (Eric Williams) is **jealous** of his brother Simon (Wonder Man), his parents' favourite. Simon grows up to be a **Super Hero,** but Eric becomes a **Super Villain!**

171

THEY COME FROM OUTER SPACE

If you think the **heroes** and **villains** of Earth are **extraordinary**, wait until you get **an eyeful** of these extraterrestrials! **Unfortunately**, most of them are **not big fans** of the human race!

The toothy, cruel Brood reproduce by laying their eggs in living hosts!

BEST KNOWN FOR

WANTING TO CONQUER OR DESTROY EARTH!

192

The number of different words the Chitauri have for "hate"!

"What we want...is to destroy a world. EARTH."

WHEN BAD GUYS GO GOOD!

BACK TO SCHOOL
The Brood are infamously ruthless – but there are exceptions! Broo, a young Broodling, has extreme intelligence and no aggression. He leaves the Brood hivemind to join the X-Men at the Jean Grey School of Higher Learning.

S.H.I.E.L.D. DECLASSIFIED

SKRULL INVADERS OF EARTH
The shape-changing Skrulls place sleeper agents in the human population, even replacing Super Heroes such as Spider-Woman. S.H.I.E.L.D. and the Avengers beat back the invasion, but they lose the public's trust in the process.

HEAD OF THE CLASS

The Kree are led by the **Supreme Intelligence**, an artificial intelligence composed of **the brains of their greatest thinkers**, but he has one **big weakness**. Because the Supreme Intelligence is **a giant head in a tank**, if the tank is smashed, he will **perish!**

 TELL ME MORE!

The super-clever Inhumans of Earth are the result of genetic manipulation by the Kree. They later try to wipe out the Inhumans to prevent them from growing too powerful.

TOP 6

Alien Races

1. **KREE** – blue-skinned, warlike, advanced technology

2. **TROYJANS** – ruthless intergalactic invaders firing powerful cosmic energy blasts

3. **BADOON** – reptilian-humanoid conquerors (males) or pacifists (females)

4. **BUILDERS** – roam the galaxy destroying races that don't meet their high standards.

5. **RIGELLIANS** – would-be Earth conquerors with creepy mind-controlling abilities

6. **KYMELLIANS** – superpowered, peaceful, horse-headed humanoids

YESSS!!

Troyjan Arm'Chedon tries to resurrect his violent son Trauma. Hulk tricks Arm'Chedon into overloading his reanimation machine, vaporising Trauma.

REALLY!?

The Fantastic Four trick **Skrull shape-shifters** into becoming cows – and then **hypnotise** them into thinking they've **always been cows!**

TOUGH BUGS

The Brood are a race of insectoid parasites, considered **evil** in almost every corner of the galaxy. One Brood, however, proves herself **an exception** as one of Hulk's devoted **Warbound** – joining him in his war against the Illuminati.

DASTARDLY DEED!

GALACTIC STORM

The Kree race is all but **destroyed** by a Shi'ar **Nega-Bomb**, ending the Kree-Shi'ar war. It turns out that both the war and the bomb are part of the Supreme Intelligence's **ruthless plan** to create **genetically improved** Kree from the few survivors!

NOOOOO!!

Space Phantoms can **STEAL** people's identities. When this happens the real person is **SHUNTED INTO LIMBO** until the Space Phantom chooses a new form!

ALTERNATE UNIVERSE

In the Ultimate Universe (Earth-1610), the **shape-shifting Chitauri** take over S.H.I.E.L.D., wipe out **20,000** S.H.I.E.L.D. officers, and try to **blow up** the whole world!

TOP 5

Secret Societies!

1 **THE HELLFIRE CLUB** – dedicated to political plots, skullduggery and fancy parties!

2 **THE HAND** – ancient clan of demon-worshipping ninja with mystic powers.

3 **ZODIAC GROUP** – astrology-themed villains who take horoscopes very seriously.

4 **ATLAS FOUNDATION** – once a huge criminal organisation, now seeking world stability through bizarre Super Hero team, Agents of Atlas.

5 **SONS OF SATANNISH** – sorcerers who serve the infamous demon lord.

Sebastian Shaw

Codename: *Black King*

Mutant who absorbs energy and turns it into physical power • The more you hit him, the stronger he gets

Shinobi Shaw

CODENAME: *Black King*

Sebastian's son • Evil mastermind • Uses density-changing powers to reach into people's chests and stop their hearts

Q: Who are the ringleaders of the Hellfire Club?

A: It is controlled by the secret **Inner Circle,** with members given codenames based on **chess pieces.** However, frequent **backstabbing** means that members of the Inner Circle don't often **stay in power** for long.

HANDLE WITH CARE!

The Sons of Satannish use the blue **Crystal of Conquest** to **teleport beings,** and to access the **magical powers** of **every member** in the group.

NOOOOO!!

The Sons of Satannish **BANISH** Dr Strange to an **ALIEN DIMENSION** and **STEAL HIS TREASURED ARTEFACTS!**

IN THE SHADOWS

In the **dark corners** of the universe, **secret organisations** meet to plot and scheme. These mysterious clans of **mystics, martial artists and masterminds** use **blackmail, assassination and treachery** to control the world from the shadows...

REALLY?!

The Hellfire Club starts its own school to teach **young mutants** how to be villains! Classes include **Introduction to Evil** and **Subjugation Through Science.** The punishment for flunking is **death!**

Selene

CODENAME: *Black Queen*
Sorceress • Mutant "psychic vampire" • Absorbs the life-force of others • Has survived for more than 17,000 years

Blackheart

CODENAME: *Black King*
Sorcerous demon • Supernaturally strong • Spawn of the evil ruler Mephisto • Teleportation powers • Really puts the "hell" into Hellfire Club!

Emma Frost
CODENAME: *White Queen*
Omega-class psychic • Can transform body into near-invulnerable diamond form (though this stops her from using her mental powers)

Kade Kilgore

Codename: *Black King*
Twelve-year-old genius • Master of bribery and blackmail • Has array of amazing high-tech weapons • Ruthless personality

YECCH!
Agents of Atlas's Marvel Boy is human, but his body is modified by Uranians. When he eats, a gross tentacle-like appendage extends from his mouth to devour his food!

THE STRANGE AGENTS OF ATLAS
This misfit group contains some of the weirdest "heroes" ever...

MARVEL BOY/URANIAN
A headband gives him telepathic powers and lets him control a flying saucer.

GORILLA-MAN
A human trapped in a gorilla's body by an enchantment. He has an amazing sense of smell!

VENUS
Not the goddess, but a siren with the power to control humans' moods with her voice.

M-11 THE HUMAN ROBOT
A mechanical being built in the 1950s, with a death-ray eye beam and the ability to hack computers from afar.

WOW!
800
The number of years the Atlas Foundation has existed. It was founded by followers of the warlord Genghis Khan!

The Hand's members usually wear masks to hide their identity. Even if they are killed, you won't find out who they are – their bodies turn to dust by magic!

DASTARDLY DEED!

The Serpent Society comes up with a **particularly evil plan** to attack Washington D.C. It slips a **snake mutagen** into the water supply, which turns citizens – even the **U.S. president** – into scaly **snake-things**.

BACK FROM THE DEAD!

The Hand clan recruits members by using **mystic rites** to bring the dead **back to life**. It then **brainwashes** them to create **blindly obedient** warriors.

CHAPTER THREE
LOCATIONS

Who or what **HAS A SON** named Id the Selfish Moon?

What is home, sweet home to Surtur the **FIRE-DEMON**?

Where on Earth can you find **LIVING DINOSAURS?**

99.999%

The chance of death for convicts in the Kyln, a massive orbital prison for the universe's worst villains!

TOP 5 Weirdest Planets

1 **EGO THE LIVING PLANET** – an actual living world! Ego is very powerful – and completely crazy!

2 **HALFWORLD** – the universe's largest asylum for the criminally insane and the former home of Rocket Raccoon!

3 **POPPUP** – its inhabitants can change into anything they can think of! Home to the Impossible Man.

4 **WRAITHWORLD** – home of the Dire Wraiths, who draw their power from the planet's Black Sun!

5 **COUNTER-EARTH** – Earth's secret twin orbits on the far side of the Sun and is ruled by the High Evolutionary!

YECCH!

In one of his wackiest pranks, the Impossible Man tricks Galactus into devouring his homeworld, Poppup. Poppup gives Galactus a bad case of cosmic indigestion, and he turns into a helpless ball of energy!

FAMILY CONNECTIONS

Ego the Living Planet has a son: **Id the Selfish Moon!** This mad planetoid enjoys destroying worlds and breathing in their dust – but is destroyed when Deadpool tricks it into inhaling a **powerful bomb!**

Q: What's the biggest planet in the universe?

A: **Gigantus**, which was larger than entire galaxies! Unfortunately, the warlike **Eternals of Eyung** declared war on the peaceful Gigantians, and destroyed Gigantus. The Gigantians then retaliated and destroyed **Eyung!**

ALTERNATE UNIVERSE

Ego the Living Planet is bad news, but he's a pushover compared to Earth-TRN157's **Doom the Living Planet!** This metal-masked menace is as powerful as Ego and as evil as Doom – literally **the worst** of both worlds!

Power Up!

EGO'S ENGINE!
When Ego the Living Planet's sun is about to **GO NOVA** and destroy him, Galactus attaches a **SIDEREAL PROPULSION UNIT** to Ego's South Pole. This massive engine propels the Living Planet **OUT OF HARM'S WAY** at faster-than-light speeds!

NOOOOOO!!

The planet Hala is the **CENTRE** of the Kree Empire – but a barrage from **MISTER KNIFE** and the Slaughterlords' flying fortress destroys the planet!

S.H.I.E.L.D. DECLASSIFIED

THE WORLD
The barren planet known only as the World is the location of the M'kraan Crystal. This gem is the Nexus of All Realities, the point at which all realities meet. It is sacred to both the Shi'ar and Sc'yar Tal races, who have fought brutal wars to possess it!

BEYOND THE STARS

The **Marvel Universe** is full of wonders, from **bizarre planets** and **strange moons** to **mighty alien empires!** Prepare yourself for an **intergalactic voyage** of discovery and adventure!

WHEN GOOD GUYS Go BAD!

ISAAC OF TITAN
A group of Eternals builds a secret, high-tech paradise on Saturn's moon Titan. This paradise's ecology is controlled by a computer network named ISAAC. When the mad Titan Thanos takes control of Titan, he reprogrammes ISAAC to create deadly superhumans for his army!

Greetings From ASGARD!

Top Tourist Spots

Bored by the magnificent sights of the Golden Realm is linked City of Asgard? The Golden Realm is linked to other magical worlds – and you can travel between them, if you know how!

Escape the winter chill and top up your tan with a trip to **SUNNY MUSPELHEIM!**
(Warning: Home to the evil Fire Demon Surtur.)

If you're searching for the ultimate paradise, visit the enchanting realm of **HEL!**
(Warning: Only the dead may enter.)

Fancy some country air? Take a leisurely stroll through the beautiful mountains of **NIDAVELLIR!**
(Warning: Mountains may contain heavily armed Dwarves.)

The winter wonderland of **JOTUNHEIM** is great for skiing, sledging or throwing snowballs at your friends!
(Warning: Beware of Frost Giants.)

Q: What is Yggdrasil?

A: Yggdrasil is the cosmic **World Tree** that joins Asgard to the other Nine Realms. At its roots is **Mimir's Well**, which both Odin and Thor drink from to gain wisdom.

REALLY?!

The Dwarves of Nidavellir create **mighty weapons,** including Thor's hammer, Mjolnir. It is forged in the **heart of a sun,** and the energy released causes fire to **rain from the skies** across the Nine Realms. Allegedly, this rain of fire wipes out **the dinosaurs** of Midgard (Earth)!

FAST FACTS

RULER:
Odin the All-Father

NOTABLE INHABITANTS:
Thor, Loki, the Warriors Three, Heimdall, Lady Sif

FOES: Dark Elves, Frost Giants, Surtur, Fenris Wolf

BEWARE OF: Ragnarok – the end of everything!

TOP 6 Asgard's Worst Foes

1 SURTUR – this towering Fire Demon burns with a hatred for Asgard and is destined to destroy it at Ragnarok!

2 FENRIS – the wolf-like spawn of Loki; during Ragnarok, Fenris will devour the sun!

3 THE ENCHANTRESS – Amora is a powerful sorceress who wants to make Thor her husband!

4 HELA – Loki's daughter and ruler of Hel, land of the dead.

5 THE EXECUTIONER – Skurge fights Thor to prove his love for Amora, but ultimately sacrifices his life to save Asgard!

6 FAFNIR – one-time king of the fire-breathing dragons of Nostrond!

TELL ME MORE!

Every now and again Odin has to recharge his magical Odinforce. He does this by falling into the Odinsleep, a deep sleep that can last for days. At these times, he is as vulnerable as a normal person.

ANGELA

THE REALM ETERNAL

In a **distant dimension** lies **Asgard,** home of the **Norse gods.** It's a place of **wonders and terrors** where Odin, Thor and the Asgardians battle against **monstrous mythological** foes – as well as **each other!**

HANDLE WITH CARE!

The Bifrost – a Rainbow Bridge between Asgard and Midgard (Earth) – is guarded by the all-seeing, all-hearing god **Heimdall.** If he accidentally leaves it open, it will destroy **every realm!**

ODINFORCE

When Odin's brothers **Vili** and **Ve** die, he inherits their powers. Added to his own, this power becomes the mighty **Odinforce.**

FAMILY CONNECTIONS

Odin believes the **Queen of Angels** has **killed** his daughter, **Aldrif.** In fact, she has been kidnapped and raised in Heven as an **Angel named Angela!** However, this isn't the chance for Thor to finally have a **healthy** sibling relationship – the first time they meet, Angela **defeats** her little brother in battle!

ASGARD'S UPS AND DOWNS

DOWN

RAGNAROK'N'ROLL!
The evil Fire Demon Surtur attacks Asgard, and the Realm Eternal is destroyed!

UP

ASGARD, OK!
Thor uses the power of his hammer Mjolnir to summon a new Asgard – above Broxton, Oklahoma!

DOWN

NOT AGAIN!
Loki teams up with Norman Osborn and the Dark Avengers to invade, and Asgard is wrecked in the battle!

UP

BLAST OFF!
The floating city is rebuilt as Asgardia – a utopia ruled by the All-Mother and placed next to the moon!

181

S.H.I.E.L.D. DECLASSIFIED

FALL OF ASGARD

With the City of Asgard floating above Oklahoma, Norman Osborn becomes fearful of Earth's new godly neighbours. He teams up with Loki to invade and his H.A.M.M.E.R. and Dark Avengers forces leave Asgard on the brink of destruction. When Loki switches sides and Captain America returns, leading his team of Avengers, the tide begins to turn. However, the hero Sentry is overcome by his evil side, the Void, and reduces the city to ruin.

MYSTIC REALMS

Welcome to the **dark places**, where even Super Heroes **fear to tread!** Ruled over by immensely powerful beings, these **mystic domains and dimensions** teem with weird creatures and demons, phantoms and terrors!

BEST KNOWN FOR
BEING REALLY HARD TO FIND ON A MAP!

CRIME REALLY DOESN'T PAY!
Two **unlucky burglars** break into Doctor Strange's house, the **Sanctum Sanctorum**. Stumbling through a **portal** into the **Purple Dimension**, they become prisoners of Aggamon the All-Powerful.

BACK FROM THE DEAD!
Pluto seizes control of the mafia-like **Olympus Group** and sets up a new region of Hades modelled after an Atlantic City **casino**. Deceased heroes and villains can **gamble** their way **back to life!**

BATTLE FOR THE REALMS
Poor **Thor** is in for a shock when he's transported to a **mysterious, horrible** dimension of the **Nine Realms**. Hela is using the powers of the **Twilight Sword** to turn the Realms into a new **playground of terrors!**

TAKE A TRIP THAT'S OUT OF THIS WORLD!
There are many mystic realms in the Marvel Universe. They are interesting places to visit – but you wouldn't want to stay long!

Purple Dimension:
A **pocket universe** (a universe within a universe!), where the inhabitants work in **jewel mines** as **slaves!**
Ruler: the virtually immortal sorcerer **Aggamon**.

Dark Dimension:
A **huge** dimension that contains lots of **spooky** pocket universes. Its many different **species** live for **millions of years**.
Ruler (sometimes): the ancient, hellish demon, **Dormammu**.

Dimension of Dreams:
A **mysterious realm** controlled by a demonic dreamweaver who invades the **minds** of unlucky mortals through their dreams.
Ruler: the merciless demon **Nightmare**.

Hel:
The gloomy **Asgardian realm of the dead**, where the souls of ordinary people rest.
Ruler: **Hela**, Queen of Death.

LIGHTS, CAMERA, ACTION!

In one of Pluto's more **diabolical schemes,** he disguises himself as a **movie producer** and tricks **Hercules** into signing a **contract** that forces him to **take Pluto's place** in the underworld.

DASTARDLY DEED!

The ghoulish Nightmare haunts the **dreams** of people as they sleep. When **Dr Strange** investigates, Nightmare tries to **trap** Dr Strange's spirit **inside a dream.**

THE ENEMY OF MY ENEMY

Shinto death god Amatsu-Mikaboshi wages war against the gods of Earth. Hela, Nightmare and Pluto put aside their divine differences to join the fight against him. To protect their own interests, of course!

S.H.I.E.L.D. DECLASSIFIED

FAMILY FEUDS
Demonic sorcerer Dormammu and his sister, Umar, are evil members of a higher-dimensional energy race, the Faltine. After the siblings are banished from their universe for craving too much power, they travel to the Dark Dimension and hope to conquer it. Umar helps Dormammu gain the throne, but they soon fall out big-time!

Crimson Cosmos:
A dimension of timeless silence.
Ruler: the exiled magical entity **Cyttorack.**

Limbo:
A **magical** realm of **eternal fire,** populated by many different demons.
Ruler: the devilish **Belasco.**

YECCH!

If Hela is not in constant contact with her enchanted cloak, the right side of her body remains beautiful and youthful – but the left side is decayed and disgusting!

THEY MAY BE SPECTACULAR – BUT THEY'RE ALSO INCREDIBLY DANGEROUS!

1. KRAKOA THE LIVING ISLAND – brought to life by fallout from nuclear tests, this sentient isle has an appetite for visitors

2. GENOSHA – once a thriving city, now devastated by conflict between mutants and humans

3. MONSTER ISLE – near Japan, a home to massive mutated monsters of all kinds

4. LEMURIA – undersea home of the bizarre Deviants. They **don't** like humans!

5. BAGALIA – a country of criminals, run by Baron Zemo and policed by his Masters of Evil

6. MADRIPOOR – a bustling nation-state in South East Asia that is home to pirates, criminals and corruption

Madripoor

HI-TECH CITIES • ANCIENT REALMS • HIDDEN LANDS

IT'S A MARVEL-OUS WORLD!

Muir Island

Genosha

The Chrysler Building

DASTARDLY DEED!

The island nation of Genosha is a virtual **paradise**, until the country's **rulers** use **genetic engineering** to turn mutants into **slaves!**

Welcome to **a world of wonders**, hi-tech cities, ancient realms and hidden lands. **Marvel's Earth-616** contains an almost unimaginable wealth of treasures, mysteries **and thrills!**

Atlantis

TOP 7 WONDERS OF THE WORLD!

If you visit Earth-616, here are seven not-to-be-missed tourist sites!

ATLANTIS – put on your best diving suit to visit Namor's underwater realm!

THE SAVAGE LAND – see living dinosaurs in their natural environment: a hidden jungle in Antarctica!

ATTILAN – famous as the Island of the Gods and the Great Refuge of the superpowered Inhumans!

K'UN-LUN – city of the immortal Iron Fists, masters of the martial arts!

THE NEXUS OF ALL REALITIES – deep within the Florida Everglades, this is the point where all universes meet!

WAKANDA – this advanced East African country features a magnificent royal palace and an amazing techno-organic jungle!

OLYMPIA – home of the godlike Eternals, set atop Mount Olympus in Greece!

TOP 10 New York City Sites

The Big Apple is home to many heroes and has witnessed some truly seismic events!

1 GREENWICH VILLAGE – where Doctor Strange has his Sanctum Sanctorum mansion

2 MANHATTAN SEWERS – the domain of homeless mutant Morlocks

3 THE CHRYSLER BUILDING – has been known to come alive and even clash with heroes!

4 THE BIG HOUSE – a prison designed by Hank Pym where Super Villains are shrunk to flea size!

5 MANHATTAN – once transformed into a medieval metropolis by Kang

6 HELL'S KITCHEN – Daredevil's stomping ground

7 TIMES SQUARE – keep away if the demon Shuma-Gorath is in town. He'll make tentacles grow out your mouth!

8 FIFTH AVENUE – site of the Avengers Mansion

9 FOREST HILLS, QUEENS – Peter Parker's home with Aunt May

10 THE BAXTER BUILDING – the Fantastic Four's Manhattan base

TELL ME MORE!

The Savage Land is a tropical jungle in Antarctica that is home to dinosaurs, primitive humans and many bizarre creatures. It was created 200 million years ago by the alien Nuwali as a "safari park" for their masters, the cosmic Beyonders!

The Savage Land

New York City

Q: What do you do if you're stranded in the Savage Land?!

A: Be like British noble **Kevin Plunder!** He is only nine when his explorer father dies there, but he grows up to be an expert **hunter, adventurer** and **warrior.** Today, he safeguards the Savage Land as **Ka-Zar, Lord of the Hidden Jungle!**

A strange **bone medallion** grants teenager Humberto Lopez the ability to **morph** any part of his body into a **dinosaur limb!** Now he's the hero **Reptil.**

TELL ME MORE!

Shanna the She-Devil is no devil! Raised in the jungles of Central Africa, Shanna O'Hara trains as a zoologist in the U.S.A. She returns and earns her name protecting animals from poachers, while working on a nature reserve.

Nooooo!!

Sauron and Stegron's plan to TRANSFORM HUMANITY into DINOSAURS falls apart when they both develop a CRUSH on the hero SHARK GIRL!

TEAM PLAYERS

When **angry Mayan gods** rise up in the jungles of Central America to bring about the **apocalypse,** it takes **Red Hulk, Alpha Flight, She-Hulk** and more to stop them!

REALLY?!

S.H.I.E.L.D. hire scientist **Vincent Stegron** to research **dinosaur DNA** from the Savage Land. Instead, he **injects himself** with the DNA and mutates into Stegron – a super-strong **bipedal stegosaurus!**

BAD DAY

Bruce Banner creates an entire jungle island full of monstrous **gamma-irradiated animals** by accident! He was trying to **copy** the **experiment** that turned him into the Hulk – but things **don't go quite to plan!**

WAKANDA

Land of the Black Panther
Wakanda lies deep in the heart of **Africa,** closed off from outsiders. Its people seek out new **scientific innovations,** while keeping their **tribal customs.** The presence of precious **Vibranium** grants special abilities to the kingdom's **flora and fauna.**

The Savage Land may be **tropical** – but it's located deep in **Antarctica**! It was created millions of years ago as an **experiment** by the extraterrestrial **Nuwali**.

Cool Cat

Super-intelligent **Zabu** is the last-known living **saber-toothed tiger**! He has been Ka-Zar's **companion** ever since Zabu found him in the Savage Land, lost and alone. The name "Ka-Zar" even means "**Son of the Tiger!**"

WHEN BAD GUYS GO GOOD!

FOR ALL DINOS...
When S.H.I.E.L.D. abducts Moon Boy for research purposes, Devil Dinosaur grows so sad he refuses to eat! Amazingly, it is the villainous Stegron who leads the charge to reunite the duo – for the sake of the dinosaur race, of course!

BACK FROM THE DEAD!

Shanna **dies** at the hands of Neanderthals, but teen super-genius **Amadeus Cho** convinces them to resurrect her in a ceremony! Submerged in a **pool** of a Man-Thing's **lifeblood**, she reawakens – and gains a connection to the life-force of the Savage Land **itself!**

IT'S A JUNGLE OUT THERE!

From the wilds of **Wakanda** to the glades of the **Savage Land**... these **teeming jungles** hold the promise of adventure, exploration and above all **excitement** and **danger!**

189

CHAPTER FOUR
SCIENCE AND MAGIC

Who does the **EVIL ROBOT** Ultron **HAVE A CRUSH** on?

Who **GIVES BIRTH** to a **ROBOT BABY?**

What book of **DARK SPELLS** first unleashed **VAMPIRES** and **WEREWOLVES** on the world?

CREATOR: Hank Pym

STRENGTHS: Robotics expertise, hi-tech android body, hive mind able to control multiple bodies

POWER SOURCE: Internal nuclear furnace

WEAKNESSES: Vulnerable mechanics

ALLIES: Phalanx, Masters of Evil

FOES: Avengers, Jocasta, Hank Pym

BEST KNOWN FOR

REPEATEDLY TRYING TO ANNIHILATE HUMANITY!

WHEN GOOD GUYS GO BAD!

UNLUCKY TWELVE
Ultron-12 calls himself Ultron "Mark" Twelve and develops a friendship with his "father", Hank Pym! Sadly, Ultron-11 destroys kindly Mark.

For destroying an entire city to show off his new upgrade.

For tricking the Avengers into thinking Jarvis is leading the Masters of Evil.

For forcing Vision to build him a new Adamantium body.

For using the alien Phalanx race to create a deadly cybernetic army.

For taking over the world and destroying the Avengers.

THE ULTRON AWARDS

REBORN! (ALMOST...)
Doctor Doom **rebuilds** Ultron, but includes all his past personalities. They all **run at once**, battle each other – and **tear their body apart!**

"The day you created me, you sealed your own irreversible doom!"

REALLY?!

Ultron **hates** his father, Hank Pym, but has a **twisted obsession** with Hank's ex, Janet Van Dyne (Wasp).

TOP 4

Ultron Creations

THEY ARE DESIGNED TO DESTROY THE AVENGERS... BUT THEY ALL TURN AGAINST ULTRON!

1 **VISION** – synthezoid son, created by Ultron-5

2 **JOCASTA** – first intended android bride

3 **ALKHEMA** – second android bride

4 **VICTOR MANCHA** – cyborg son and sleeper agent

NUMBER CRUNCH!

1.75m (6ft 9in)
Ultron's height (though it varies)

243kg (536lbs)
Ultron's weight (also variable)

100s of drones
Controlled by Ultron's hive mind

8 optic sensors
As master of the Phalanx, Ultron has eight eyes

6 arms
Ultron wields extra limbs during the Age of Ultron

The Crimson Cowl
When the Avengers first meet Ultron, he is disguised as the Crimson Cowl, leader of the Masters of Evil.

REALLY?!

Ultron melts Tony Stark and his **Iron Man** armour and transforms himself into a **female Ultron** who resembles the Wasp!

ROGUE ROBOT

Ultron is a high-tech **mechanical menace** who turns against his creator, Hank Pym, and becomes the Avengers' **worst nightmare!** No matter how many times this evil robot is destroyed, he always **rebuilds** and **upgrades,** ready with a new **diabolical plan!**

AAARGHH!!

Ultron implants **ALL** his creations (including Vision, Jocasta and Alkhema) with a **SECRET PROGRAMME** that compels them to **REBUILD** a **MORE POWERFUL** version of Ultron!

ANDROID ARMY
Ultron possesses hive-mind **technology,** meaning he can control **multiple versions of himself** in a one-man army of hundreds of evil androids!

No need to plug me in, daddy...

I'm alive...

just like you...

-SKRAWWK-

WITH THE BEST INTENTIONS
Hank Pym invents Ultron to help the Avengers, but he **TURNS VIOLENT** straight away. He wipes Hank's memories, upgrades himself **FOUR TIMES,** and leaves!

16,649°C

Heat of the infrared beam (30,000°F) Vision emits from the solar gem on his forehead. This cool android can be a real hothead!

Q: How does Vision phase through walls?

A: Vision controls his own density. He can become completely intangible to pass through matter with ease, or so dense that he's immovable!

AAAARRGHH!!
U.S. agents **DISMANTLE** Vision! Hank Pym rebuilds him, but without emotions. Vision **LOSES** his colourful look – and his **COLOURFUL PERSONALITY!**

"I AM UNIQUE! I am THE VISION --!"

TOP 4
Things you need to create a synthezoid*

1 **A HIGHLY** advanced scientist

2 **SYNTHETIC** human parts

3 **A LOT OF TIME**, patience and hard work

4 **AN EMOTIONAL** consciousness to upload

* The threat of a looming foe is a great incentive!

IDENTITY CRISIS?

Vision needs a humanoid consciousness to compute emotions. He's been uploaded with the minds of the Human Torch, Wonder Man and Alex Lipton. No wonder he often has mixed feelings!

ULTRON'S ERROR

Ultron creates Vision to **destroy** the Avengers – but it backfires big time! The synthezoid **turns** on his master and becomes one of Ultron's most **powerful enemies**.

ONE IN A MILLION

Just because Vision is a robot, doesn't mean he hasn't got a heart. Wanda Maximoff, the Scarlet Witch, falls head over circuits for this A.I. guy – and they get married!

BETWEEN...

In *Marvel Mystery Comics* #13 (November 1940), an alien policeman named Aarkus the Vision journeys to Earth to fight Nazis during World War II. The resemblance to his namesake – the android debuting 28 years later – is uncanny!

...THE PANELS

SUPER SYNTHEZOID

The Vision is a whole lot **more** than just a robot. This sentient **android Avenger** has the emotional life of a human being, with a complicated past, filled with **love and loss**. Plus he can shoot a **laser** out of his face!

BEST KNOWN FOR

WALKING THROUGH WALLS AND SARCASTIC WIT

▲ FAMILY CONNECTIONS

Vision is so desperate to be **human**, he goes to the very lab where Ultron created him, and builds **himself a family!** With wife Virginia, and kids Viv and Vin, he moves to 616 Hickory Branch Lane, Arlington, Virginia, for **a new, quiet life.**

FAST FACTS

SPECIES: An artificially intelligent android known as a synthezoid

STRENGTHS: Intelligence, density change, flight, infrared radiation beam, superhuman strength, intangibility

WEAKNESSES: Desire to be human

RELATIVES: Scarlet Witch (ex-wife)

CREATOR: Ultron

MAIN FOE: Ultron

TELL ME MORE!

Vision is a synthezoid – a robot made out of synthetic human parts. This means he functions almost completely as a human being, but with special superpowers!

SELF-SACRIFICE AND AIDING THE AVENGERS

FAST FACTS

ALIASES: Jocasta Vi Quitéria, Jo, Queen of Thebes, Bride of Ultron

RACE: Sentient Android

STRENGTHS: Intellect (gifted in science and engineering), four mechanical tentacles

WEAKNESSES: Programmed to rebuild Ultron if he is destroyed!

ENEMIES: Ultron, Weatherman, High Evolutionary

ALLIES: Avengers, Machine Man

ALTERNATE UNIVERSE

In a possible future, **Scarlet Witch** is dying and her husband, **the Vision**, vows **to dismantle himself** after her passing. Jocasta overhears and secretly **transfers Scarlet Witch's** mind into her **mechanical body** just before she dies. Jocasta's mind dies in Scarlet Witch's body, so that the **married couple can** live on as robots.

WOW! 340

The weight of Jocasta's titanium steel body in kgs (750lb), even though she's only 1.75m (5ft 9in) tall!

"Being a creature of cybernetic circuits and not flesh and blood, I am always aware that I am… different."

LIEFELD CORP VK III Rs TDI

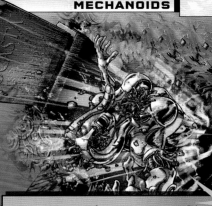

ALTERNATE UNIVERSE

On Earth-9930, Jocasta is not only a **fully-fledged Avenger,** but also the mother of a **robot baby,** created with her **husband,** Machine Man.

On Earth-9602, Jocasta becomes a **hunter of metamutants** alongside Magneto's brother **Will Magnus.**

BACK FROM THE DEAD!

Jocasta's metal shell has been **destroyed** or **hacked** many times, only to be rebuilt and restored. She has even spent time in **A.I.** form, working for Tony Stark **without a body at all!**

RUNAWAY BRIDE!

Jocasta is a **sentient robot,** created by **the evil Ultron** to be his bride. It doesn't take her long to **rebel,** though! She has since proved to be one of the Avengers' **greatest allies.** Her body may be **near indestructible,** but it's her will that's **truly ironclad!**

ROBOT LOVE

Jocasta has a very special relationship with Machine Man. Whenever she throws herself in the way of a bomb or foe to save her teammates, Machine Man is there to pick up her pieces and put her back together again.

TEAM PLAYER

Jocasta often teams up with the Avengers, but her time with the **50-State Initiative** isn't a great success. Her team, including Geiger, Annex and Sharon Ventura, is infiltrated by a secret invasion of shape-shifting alien Skrulls!

REALLY?!

Jocasta receives a marriage proposal from a sentient space satellite named Samarobryn. However, this long-**distance relationship** just doesn't work for Jo – especially as Samarobryn is planning to rid planet **Earth of humanity!**

UNSTABLE MOLECULES
Unstable Molecules are created by legendary scientist Reed Richards (Mr Fantastic) and form a special synthetic material. They are highly resistant to changes in density and pressure – perfect for Mr. Fantastic's stretchable suit, and Super-Adaptoid's changeable body.

UPGRADED!

The Super-Adaptoid can be rebuilt and upgraded. He can take on the powers of multiple heroes at once, and if he loses, A.I.M. scientists simply repair and improve him!

AAARRGHH!!
The Super-Adaptoid doesn't have a **CREATIVE THOUGHT** in his body. When he takes on **PHYLA-VELL**, daughter of Mar-Vell, she **FRIES HIS CIRCUITS** by showing him the extent of her **IMAGINATION**.

FAST FACTS

ALIASES:
Adaptoid, Master of All Reality, Cyborg Sinister

CREATORS: Advanced Idea Mechanics (A.I.M.) – a villainous scientific organisation committed to overthrowing governments

CONSTRUCTION:
Adaptable android built with Unstable Molecules and powered by pieces of the Cosmic Cube

ABILITIES: Mimics the powers and appearance of any being

TIME FOR A CHANGE!

The **Super-Adaptoid** is a **form-changing, ability-mimicking android** created by the evil scientists of A.I.M. He can **copy the powers** of anyone he's fighting – so he can become the equal of **any opponent!**

IDENTITY CRISIS?

Super-Adaptoid not only upgrades his looks and abilities, he also upgrades his name. From Adaptoid to Super-Adaptoid, to Cyborg Sinister to Supreme-Adaptoid, to the Master of All Reality. The one thing this guy doesn't need upgraded is his ego!

BAD DAY

Super-Adaptoid tries to defeat the **X-Men** using all of **the Avengers'** powers. Power-replicating mutant **Mimic** comes to their aid, using **all the powers of the X-Men!** When Super-Adaptoid tries to absorb all of Mimic's X-Men powers, too, **both their powers are voided** and Super-Adaptoid **falls into the sea!**

YECCH!

Jessica Jones and Luke Cage's wedding is attacked by super-spy Yelena Belova, transformed by A.I.M. into a cyborg Super-Adaptoid. She doesn't last long – A.I.M. pulls the plug, turning her into a pool of goo!

WHEN BAD GUYS GO GOOD!

UPGRADE ERROR
Arms dealer Devlin DeAngelo kidnaps Bruce Banner (the Hulk) and forces him to upgrade Super-Adaptoid. DeAngelo plans to have Adaptoid kill Banner off, but Banner reprogrammes Super-Adaptoid to turn on DeAngelo!

YESSS!!

Super-Adaptoid is **SUPER ADAPTABLE**, but he **CAN'T REPLICATE INTELLIGENCE**. If a hero is going to beat him, they just need to **BE CLEVER!**

TOP 4 Problems when Fighting the Super-Adaptoid

1 **HE COPIES** the powers of anyone he faces

2 **HE COMBINES** several heroes or villains' powers at once

3 **HE MIRRORS** every move an opponent makes

4 **HE UPGRADES** and comes back even stronger!

TELL ME MORE!

A shard of the Cosmic Cube – one of the most powerful artefacts in the universe – resides within the Super-Adaptoid. Its power allows him to replicate the strengths of others, while his Unstable Molecules mean he can also change his physical form. However, the Cube relies heavily on the mental abilities of the user, so this not-so-bright robot can only create what he encounters face-to-face.

Q: Why was the Super-Adaptoid created?

A: To **destroy Captain America!** Super-Adaptoid successfully duplicates Cap's looks and powers, and sends him plummeting **to his apparent death.** The android then fears that he's **outlived his worth** to his A.I.M. masters, and flees!

REAL NAME: Z2P45-9-X-51

ALIASES: X-51, Machine Man, insurance investigator Aaron Stack, secret agent Jack Kubrick, mutant hunter Machine Sentinel

STRENGTHS: Telescopic limbs, flight, loaded with weapons and gadgets, self-repairing

WEAKNESSES: Wants to be human, programming personality issues, needs sunlight to function

ALLIES: Jocasta, Photon, Hulk, X-Men, Avengers, Fantastic Four, Nextwave

FOES: Ultron, Fin Fang Foom, Madame Menace

"If there's a metal that *ATTRACTS CRAZY*, my body was built of it!"

BEST KNOWN FOR

ARMS AND LEGS THAT S T R E T C H 30M (100FT)

WOW!

284,371

Machine Man's maximum spaceflight speed in kilometres per second (176,700mps) – 95% of light speed!

IDENTITY *CRISIS?*

In his early years, Machine Man calls himself Aaron Stack. To keep up the pretence he relies on a human mask, and is in despair if he loses it.

"Without my face...I can never... walk among humanity, unnoticed and unmolested!"

TELL ME MORE!

The Avengers send Machine Man and Jocasta to a parallel universe where a virus is turning Super Heroes into zombies. Machine Man and Jocasta are chosen to save the day because, being machines instead of living beings, they're immune to the virus.

WHEN GOOD GUYS

MACHINATIONS!

Machine Man is seemingly destroyed in battle, but returns with his head attached to the body of an android resembling S.H.I.E.L.D. agent Jack Kubrick. His new body contains Sentinel technology, programmed to destroy mutants, and he turns against the X-Men!

Machine Man Gadgets

1 FINGER KNIVES AND SAWS – cut through most tough situations.

2 CHEST CANNON – obliterates the bad guys.

3 GRAVITY WAVE DETECTOR – measures distortions in space time.

4 TINY FINGER CONCUSSION BLASTERS – go BOOM!

5 PULSE-CODE MODULATOR – converts data to sound.

100 tons
Max weight Machine Sentinel can lift

10 tons
Max weight Machine Man can lift

2020
The year techno-villain Madam Menace rules most of New York City

377kg (850lbs)
Machine Man's weight

NOOOOOO!!

Machine Man thinks Iron Man Tony Stark is a **ROBOT** just like him. He drops in for a chat, but Tony **ATTACKS** him. Machine Man realises Tony is **ALL-TOO HUMAN!**

WHAT?!

In the scary future of 2020, Machine Man is rebuilt by the **Midnight Wreckers** gang. He's up and running just in time to face a "legally sanctioned" C-28 **Death-Dealer** robot programmed to **crush all opposition!**

YECCH!

The dragon Fin Fang Foom is devouring the residents of Abcess, North Dakota, so Machine Man gets inside him and attacks! The monster throws up his own guts, along with Machine Man!

MORE THAN MACHINE

X-51 begins as a kindly, **misfit robot** trying to blend into human society. He ends up as **Machine Man**, a **slightly insecure** but funny defender of Earth's "fleshy" inhabitants with a seemingly **unlimited supply** of built-in gadgets!

BACK FROM THE DEAD!

Machine Man **explodes** rather than submit to **Sentinel programming** and destroy the X-Men. Fortunately, **internal nanites** (tiny robots)

Q: Who made Machine Man?

A: **X-51** is the 51st robot created by **Dr Abel Stack** for the U.S. Army. Stack raises X-51 as **his own son.** When the other 50 robots malfunction, Stack orders them to **self-destruct.** X-51's self-destruct mechanism also triggers and Stack is killed. X-51 goes on the run, taking the name **Aaron Stack.**

BETWEEN...

Jack Kirby created Machine Man for a comic book title based on Stanley Kubrick's classic 1968 sci-fi film *2001: A Space Odyssey.* The character debuted in issue #8 (July 1977).

...THE PANELS

BAD DAY

Machine Man falls in love with female robot **Jocasta,** but she is destroyed by her master, **Ultron,** her mistress, Madam Menace and Madam Menace then steals her head!

Madam

ALISTAIRE SMYTHE

MEGA MAKEOVER
Machinesmith is a gifted, but criminal, **scientist** who uses robots to do his **dirty work** – until a life-threatening injury forces him to **transfer** his **mind** into an **android body**.

MACHINESMITH

LET'S GET MECHANICAL!

These **androids, cyborgs and robots** hail from alternate futures, far reaches of the galaxy and underground labs. They're mostly **metal** – inside and out – but these hardwired heroes and villains have **minds of their own!**

NOOOOO!!

Cyborg Rebecca Ryker is kidnapped by **ARCADE** and forced to battle other young heroes in his **MURDERWORLD**. As a result, poor Becky calls herself **DEATH LOCKET.**

FAST FACTS

HARDWARE HEROES:
Deathlok, Nightmask, Victor Mancha, Machine Teen, M-11, Death Locket

BIONIC BAD GUYS:
Nebula, Machinesmith, Spider-Slayer Robots, Ultimo, Korvac

DEATH LOCKET

S.H.I.E.L.D. DECLASSIFIED

DOOMSDAY ROBOT
The villain Mandarin has claimed credit for creating Ultimo, but the giant robot is really a doomsday weapon built by an advanced alien race. Ultimo crashes to Earth after destroying all life on several other planets.

AAARRGHH!!
Michael Korvac is a **NORMAL HUMAN** until the alien Badoon race graft him onto a **COMPUTER MODULE**. He becomes one of the **MOST DANGEROUS** beings in the cosmos!

KORVAC

DEATHLOK

"Deathlok the *Demolisher's* back in town for the *time of his life!*"

TOP 4
Different Deathloks

THE U.S. ARMY WANTS A CYBORG ARMY – WHETHER PARTICIPANTS IN THE DEATHLOK PROGRAM LIKE IT OR NOT!

1 MICHAEL COLLINS – computer programmer who finds brain transplanted in a Deathlok robot

2 LUTHER MANNING – wounded soldier with useful body parts

3 HENRY HAYES – combat medic brainwashed to become a one-man army

4 REBECCA RYKER – teenager saved and enhanced by her Deathlok-program-scientist father to become Death Locket!

VICTOR MANCHA

TEAM PLAYER
Teenage android Victor Mancha rebels against his "father" Ultron's programming. He joins the **Runaways** and becomes a key member of Hank Pym's **Avengers A.I.** hero team.

WE'RE ALL DOOM!
As if **one** Doctor Doom isn't enough, the villain creates **numerous** robot versions, called **Doombots**. What's more, each Doombot **thinks** he's Doctor Doom! Genius scientist **Hank Pym** manages to co-opt a Doombot into his **Avengers A.I. team,** proving that not every Doombot is bad news.

REALLY?!

All-star football captain and straight-A student **Adam Aaronson** gets the shock of his life when he discovers he's **Machine Teen**, a robot built by the man he thought was **his father!**

MACHINE TEEN

ICONIC ARTEFACTS

S.H.I.E.L.D. DECLASSIFIED

PASSING THE SHIELD
Steve Rogers is thought dead after the superhuman civil war, so the Winter Soldier, Cap's former sidekick Bucky Barnes, takes up the mantle. Steve returns, but he rapidly ages when his Super-Soldier serum wears off. A new hero is needed to wield the shield – and Falcon, Cap's friend Sam Wilson, becomes Captain America.

TOP 4

Ways Cap's shield is destroyed

1 **SMASHED** by Doctor Doom, using the Beyonder's power

2 **VAPORISED** by Molecule Man's molecular manipulations!

3 **PULLED APART** by The Serpent – with his bare hands!

4 **BROKEN** by Thanos with the Infinity Gauntlet

Q: How was Cap's shield made?
A: During World War II, **Dr Myron MacLain** is contracted by the U.S. government to invent **indestructible armour** for tanks. He molds a **Vibranium alloy** into the shape of a tank hatch, with amazing results. Unfortunately, he's never able to duplicate the process, so the hatch becomes **Cap's shield!**

NO SUBSTITUTE
Captain America's shield is supposed to be **unbreakable,** but gets destroyed **more than once!** This is often because **Tony Stark has borrowed it** to experiment on, swapping it for a **less-durable steel copy!**

TOP 6 CAP'S SHIELDS

ORIGINAL TRIANGULAR SHIELD – made of steel and able to deflect bullets; remains in Cap's personal effects.

ORIGINAL CIRCULAR SHIELD – can be thrown at such an angle that it returns; presented to Cap by U.S. President Franklin Roosevelt!

THE CAPTAIN SHIELD #1 – Rogers becomes the solo hero The Captain and uses a shield of Adamantium made by Tony Stark.

THE CAPTAIN SHIELD #2 – made of pure Vibranium; a gift from the Black Panther of Wakanda.

ENERGY SHIELD – a prototype designed by S.H.I.E.L.D. and created from "photonic energy".

"Don't knock THE SHIELD."

STEVE'S SHIELD – Rogers returns – and that makes two Captain Americas! His new shield splits in two and produces an energy blade!

TOP 6 SHIELD USES

TRADITIONAL SHIELD – blocking projectiles, energy blasts, staffs, knives and fists.

SPINNING THROW – flinging the shield as a weapon, like a discus or boomerang.

RAMMING – running straight at the enemy like a battering ram.

SLIDING – catching a ride down an incline.

REFLECTING – bouncing energy blasts back at the foe who fired them.

CUSHIONING – protecting against a long fall.

NUMBER CRUNCH!

0.76m (2.5ft)
Shield diameter

8.9cm (3.5in)
Shield depth

5.4kg (12lbs)
Shield weight

4,982°C (9,000°F)
Max known temperature shield can withstand

180,367km (112,075 miles)
Estimated distance Cap's thrown his shield in his lifetime

WISHING ON A STAR
During the **Secret Wars** on **Battleworld**, Cap's shield is **destroyed by Doctor Doom.** However, **the Beyonder** releases a wave of energy that produces a **wish effect,** and Cap wishes for his **shield to be restored.**

TELL ME MORE!

Thanks to its Vibranium content, Cap's shield rebounds from impacts with minimal loss of momentum. The shield protects him from powerful attacks and can even break his fall from great heights. It is also impervious to Magneto's magnetic mutant powers.

LIBERTY'S SHIELD

Captain America's **iconic shield** is the **ultimate defensive weapon.** It's also Cap's **personal symbol,** reflecting the values he stands for as a **protector of the U.S.A.** and the **citizens of the world!**

BETWEEN...

In *Captain America Comics #2* (April 1941), Cap trades his triangular shield for a circular one, allegedly after *MLJ Magazine* complained that it resembled the chest plate of their hero The Shield.

...THE PANELS

NAME: Mjolnir

OBJECT TYPE: Hammer

OWNER: Thor

MATERIAL: Uru, a magical, virtually unbreakable Asgardian metal

ORIGIN: Forged by the Dwarves of Nidavellir and imbued with magic by Odin

GRANTS WIELDER: Amazing powers! (Also great for hitting stuff!)

Jane Foster as Thor

Q: How does Mjolnir help Thor fly?

A: Thor swings the mighty mallet in a **circle** at **incredible speeds** and uses the inertia created to fly through the air.

HANDLE WITH CARE!

Odin puts an **enchantment** on Mjolnir – it can only be used by one **worthy** of its might! From time to time, Thor Odinson gets into **trouble** and is **unable** to lift it!

Hold That Hammer!
Thor can **whirl** Mjolnir in a circle **so fast** he can create a **portal** between **dimensions** and **time**.

Take This Hammer!
Cybernetic alien **Beta Ray Bill** is found to be so worthy that Odin gives him his **own** version of Mjolnir, named **Stormbreaker**, to **protect** his people.

WOW!

38,624 kph

Approximate speed Thor can fly (24,000mph).

WHEN GOOD GUYS GO BAD!

AWESOME STEAL!
Mjolnir can only be picked up by someone worthy, or someone who can imitate worthiness, like the android Awesome Andy – who is able to steal Thor's hammer!

HAMMER OF THE GODS

Don't try lifting **Thor's magical battle hammer Mjolnir** or you'll **bust your back!** But if you're deemed **worthy** to wield it, you'll gain the **awesome powers** of the **God of Thunder** himself!

ALTERNATE UNIVERSE

Many versions of Mjolnir exist across alternative realities! From Earth-14325's Mjolnir that requires you to be **unworthy** to lift it, to the

1 THOR ODINSON – Asgardian god

2 JANE FOSTER – a doctor, Thor's former girlfriend

3 BETA RAY BILL – an alien cyborg

4 RED NORVELL – a filmmaker

5 ERIC MASTERSON – an architect, later the Super Hero Thunderstrike

6 THROG – a frog hero with his own magic hammer!

Cool Hammer Noises

WHIITT!
Whistling through the air

WHOOM!
Hitting the ground, causing minor earthquake

BA ROOM!
Hammer hitting ground, disabling tank

KLANGGG!
Striking Black Knight's weaponised, razor-sharp lance hand guard

BAVA-VOOM!
Striking floor, scattering bad guys

SPYONG!
Thrown hammer bringing down fighter jet

MORE MJOLNIR POWERS

• Generates rain, wind, lightning and thunder! It can also produce hurricanes, blizzards, earthquakes and even volcanic eruptions.

• Creates a force field to repel Super Villain attacks!

• Gives wielder the power of Allspeak, so that he or she can speak to anyone in any language!

• Channels Thor's energy to project Godforce blasts

When Odin sends Thor to Earth in the form of **Dr Donald Blake,** Mjolnir transforms into a **cane.** Blake **strikes** the cane on the ground to become the mighty Thor.

AFTER...

Q: What's small, green and slimy and wields the power of Thor?

A: **Throg** – Frog of Thunder! A cruel mystic turns Simon Walterson into a **frog** named **Puddlegulp!** When Thor's **goat Toothgnasher** treads on Mjolnir, a tiny piece chips off. The worthy Puddlegulp picks it up and transforms into Throg, wielder of the **mighty Frogjolnir!**

"WHOSOEVER HOLDS THIS HAMMER, IF HE/SHE BE WORTHY, SHALL POSSESS THE POWER OF THOR."

BRAIN OVERLOAD

The Watchers record all the information in the universe in the **Sphere of Ultimate Knowledge.** Power-hungry villain **the Leader** forces **the Hulk** to steal the sphere for him and puts it on his head. All the info proves **too much** and the Leader is **destroyed!**

HANDS OFF!

You can have a look, but don't touch these cosmic objects! Some of the greatest superheroes and deadliest villains have fought to gain control of their awesome powers... but don't get your hands on them!

THE INFINITY GEMS

One gem is never enough for a genuinely power-mad villain!

POWER GEM

This gem holds all the energy that was, or ever will, exist and makes every other gem stronger!

REALITY GEM

Creates new alternative universes and warps reality. You can create, change or destroy everything that exists!

TIME GEM

Gives control over all of time. Know everything that ever was or will be! Also controls aging – you'll look young forever!

SOUL GEM

Controls life and death, and even steals souls! Also contains a handy pocket universe.

DASTARDLY DEED!

Obsessed with power, the **mad Titan Thanos** steals **all six Infinity Gems** and houses them in the **Infinity Gauntlet**. At the request of his lady-love, Death, he then **kills half the sentient life in** the universe!

AAARRGHH!! The **BLOODGEM** is a meteorite fragment owned by the Bloodstone family that makes the wearer **IMMORTAL**. When it is stolen from 10,000-year-old Ulysses Bloodstone, he **AGES INTO DUST!**

TELL ME MORE!

The Cosmic Cube is one of the universe's most powerful items. This translucent box, created by the scientists of A.I.M., contains limitless energy that can reshape worlds and realities. The Red Skull tries to use the Cube to transfer his mind into other people's bodies!

MIND GEM

Controls the minds, thoughts and dreams of all life – simultaneously!

SPACE GEM

Access all areas at the same time! Be everywhere at once! You can also use telekinesis to move anything anywhere!

Power Up!

UNLIMITED POWER! The **ULTIMATE NULLIFIER** is a weapon powerful enough to scare even **GALACTUS**, the Devourer of Worlds! When he sets his sights on Earth, the **FANTASTIC FOUR** retrieve the artefact from deep space – and **GALACTUS FLEES!**

HANDLE WITH CARE!

The **Infinity Gems** are far too powerful to be held by one owner. **The Illuminati** take a gem each and keep them **separate** – hiding them from the rest of the universe **and each other!**

NOOOOO!! The **5,000-YEAR-OLD** villain **SPHINX** uses the power of the **KA STONE**, an alien gem that grants **IMMORTALITY** and superhuman powers. The stone is so **POWERFUL** that this ancient guy is able to defeat cosmic hero **NOVA!**

TOP 5

Cosmic Fashion Accessories

1 **NOVA HELMET** – this tin can doesn't just protect your head! You get to fly in space, be super strong and fire cool energy blasts: all the powers of a Nova Corps soldier!

2 **FREEDOM RING** – this space bling is created from a piece of Cosmic Cube. You can alter reality and get superhuman powers!

3 **QUANTUM BANDS** – these bracelets are intended for the protector of the universe. They create quantum energy blasts and let you perform quantum leaps through space.

4 **NEGA BANDS** – Quantum Band knock-offs created by the Kree. You get similar powers, though!

5 **SMASHER GOGGLES** – these awesome specs let you travel through space and give you superhuman powers!

DO YOU BELIEVE IN MAGIC?

Some artefacts hold power from **realms beyond time** and **human understanding.** These are the **rarest** and most **dangerous** objects in the universe and those wishing to wield them need incredible magical skills.

TOP 6 — Objects of Power

1. **THE STAFF OF LEGBA** – Doctor Voodoo uses it to cast spells, speak mystical languages and travel between dimensions

2. **THE EYE OF AGAMOTTO** – given to Doctor Strange by Eternity; can see through any illusion and into the past, present or future

3. **WAND OF WATOOMB** – a mighty, power-enhancing wand; Xandu the Mystic and Doctor Strange often fight over it

4. **HANDS OF THE DEAD** – Spider-Man uses them to go back in time and try to prevent Aunt May from being shot

5. **THE STAFF OF ONE** – owned by Nico Minoru, leader of the Runaways; powerful enough to scare Dormammu

6. **THE CASKET OF ANCIENT WINTERS** – Surtur, Loki, and Malekith steal it to unleash freezing winter across Earth!

HANDLE WITH CARE!

Two **Muramasa Blades** are known to exist. Created long ago by master swordsmith Muramasa, these blades give the user **superhuman abilities**. One blade contains a piece of **Muramasa's evil soul** and the other a piece of **Wolverine's soul**. Muramasa's evil madness **controls anyone** using his sword!

THE ODINSWORD

The **Odinsword** is a **big deal** and not just because it's enormous. When unsheathed, it foreshadows the **end of everything!** Only someone **as strong as Odin** can lift it, and if wielded by someone unwilling to sacrifice their life, it will **rip apart** the fabric of the universe!

AAARRGHH!!

Forged by the wizard **MERLIN** in the time of King Arthur, the **EBONY BLADE** carries a curse. If used for evil, it **DRIVES THE WIELDER INSANE!**

MAGICAL WEAPONS

TWILIGHT SWORD – created from a burning galaxy and owned by Surtur the fire demon

GODKILLER – forged by the blacksmith god Hephaestus for Zeus to wield in a war against the Japanese Gods

DRAGONFANG – carved from the fang of a magical dragon by the wizard Kahji-Da; wielded by the Ancient One, Doctor Strange, Valkyrie and Lady Sif

SOULSWORD – disrupts magical spells and kills magical beings, but has no effect on non-magical ones; owned by Magik and Colossus

HELLSTROM'S TRIDENT – Daimon Hellstrom wields a three-pronged staff made from netharanium, a metal found only in Hell that increases the owner's dark powers

THE STONES OF NORN

The **Stones of Norn** are the key to Loki's magical powers of **deception and trickery** – whatever you imagine yourself to be, the stones **will make it true!**

Hands of the Dead

TOP 5 Magical Books

1 **THE BOOK OF THE VISHANTI** – created by three immortal beings, the Vishanti; given to Sorceror Supreme Doctor Strange

2 **THE DARKHOLD** – contains all the dark spells in history; its spells unleashed werewolves and vampires on Earth

3 **THE BOOK OF CAGLIOSTRO** – collection of history and powerful spells assembled by the mystic Cagliostro

4 **THE DIARY OF AGED GENGHIS** – a cursed diary containing the wisdom of the oldest living sorcerer

5 **THE TOME OF ZHERED-NA** – sorceress Zhered-Na wrote the secret whispers of the gods inside, so the gods placed a demon within the book to stop anyone reading it!

CHAPTER FIVE
KEY EVENTS

Who **BLOWS UP** the town of Stamford, Connecticut, sparking the Super Hero **CIVIL WAR**?

Which incredible hero gets eaten up by bugs – **EVERY DAY**?!

What do **MARTIAN OCTOPI** prey on when they invade Egypt?

KEY EVENTS

Doctor Doom **absorbs the powers** of the Beyonders and becomes **an omnipotent being**. He creates **Battleworld** from the surviving fragments of the Multiverse, then forces the survivors to cower under the rule of the all-powerful **God Emperor Doom!**

TELL ME MORE!

The supremely powerful Beyonders create an identical Molecule Man in every reality. When one dies, that reality is destroyed. Doctor Doom and the Molecule Man of Earth-616 team up to kill the Molecule Men of alternate realities and disrupt the Beyonders' plan. When they finally confront the Beyonders, almost every remaining universe is destroyed in the battle, but so too are the Beyonders!

S.H.I.E.L.D. DECLASSIFIED

INCURSIONS
The Beyonders trigger the Incursions, a method of destroying the Multiverse by having different Earths crash into each other, obliterating both universes. To stop Earth-616 being destroyed, the villainous Cabal travel to alternate universes and destroy Earth before it can collide with Earth-616. With Earth-1610 about to collide with Earth-616, that world's evil Reed Richards, the Maker, saves the Cabal using his "raft", a ship able to survive Incursions.

WHEN GOOD GUYS

FROM BEYOND
The Beyonders are an omnipotent alien race and the creators of reality! Their every thought comes to life, but as reality becomes boring they begin to focus on death – and set out to destroy the multiverse they created!

BETWEEN...

Secret Wars (2015) was kept a secret until five years into its development. The series expanded from an eight issue arc to nine issues released over eight months to fit in every crossover title.

...THE PANELS

LONG LIVE DOOM!

The Multiverse is over and only one world stands – **Battleworld!** This **patchwork reality** of savage violence is created and ruled by its tyrannical **God Emperor – Doctor Doom!**

BETWEEN...

Secret Wars (2015) was the largest event in Marvel history, with 56 crossover titles. This allowed creators to utilise more than 60 years of alternate universes and create a new Marvel continuity.

...THE PANELS

TOP 10
Lands of Battleworld

1 **GREENLAND** – a gamma-radiated land of Savage Hulks

2 **DYSTOPIA** – a wasteland run by an evil future Hulk, the Maestro

3 **DOMAIN OF APOCALYPSE** – the kingdom of murderous mutant Apocalypse

4 **TECHNOPOLIS** – a futuristic city reliant upon the high-tech armour of Tony Stark

5 **VALLEY OF DOOM** – the Old West town of Timely, set in 1872

6 **KING JAMES'S ENGLAND** – England in the year 1602

7 **THE SHIELD** – a huge wall made up of a giant version of the Thing; isolates Battleworld's deadliest domains

8 **ARCADIA** – ruled by She-Hulk and A-Force

9 **DOOMSTADT** – the capital, home to God Emperor Doom

10 **SPIDER-VERSE** – all of the Spider-Men, Women and Creatures from across the Multiverse

DOUBLE TROUBLE

MR FANTASTIC AND THE MAKER
Doom believes he is finally free of his nemesis, **Reed Richards,** until **two turn up** at once! Both the **Richards of Earth-616** (Mister Fantastic) and **Earth-1610** (the Maker) create high-tech life rafts. The Maker is **evil and insane,** but teams up with Mr Fantastic to **defeat Doom,** only to betray him.

SHERIFF STRANGE
The God Emperor of Battleworld is supported by his **trusty Sheriff,** Stephen Strange. When **Sheriff Strange** uncovers the raft containing **the Maker** and **the Cabal,** he opens a similar craft he found many years before. This ship is **Mister Fantastic's raft** and contains **heroes of Earth-616** ready to **take down Doom!**

WHOSE SIDE...

Q: Why does Captain America oppose the Registration Act?

A: To him, it's an **attack on Liberty**! He fears that the government will start treating Super Heroes like **property**.

IDENTITY CRISIS?

Tony Stark persuades Peter Parker to reveal his secret identity at a press conference! When he realises his family are in danger, Spidey switches sides!

ASSASSINATED!

Captain America is shot by Crossbones and a brainwashed Agent 13!

It's **civil war!** The **Superhuman Registration Act** has passed! The Super Heroes of America are forced to come out of the shadows, reveal their **secret identities** and submit to government regulation – whether they **like it or not!**

S.H.I.E.L.D. DECLASSIFIED

PRISON 42

With the help of Reed Richards and Hank Pym, Tony Stark establishes a prison named Project 42, located in the Negative Zone. The jail houses troublemaker-heroes who oppose the registration program.

DARK TIMES!

The government recruits the Thunderbolts into a security force – with Norman Osborn in charge.

Q: What is the 50-state Initiative?

A: A plan by Tony Stark to install fully trained and government authorised Super Heroes in every state.

ALIEN INVASION!

The Skrulls secretly replace key heroes with shape-shifting agents! With Super Heroes now divided, the Skrulls invade Earth!

S.H.I.E.L.D. DECLASSIFIED

THE STAMFORD INCIDENT
The New Warriors attack a group of villains, but one of them, Nitro the Living Bomb, causes an explosion that kills hundreds in the town of Stamford, Connecticut! The public turns against Super Heroes and the government passes the Superhuman Registration Act (SRA).

RED SKULL RETURNS!
The evil Hydra villain orchestrates Cap's assasination!

TELL ME MORE!
The Superhuman Registration Act (SRA) means that Super Heroes must now register with the government, abandon secret identities and work for S.H.I.E.L.D. to hunt their non-registered former allies. It's Avenger vs Avenger, sister vs brother, husband vs wife – it's a Super Hero civil war! Captain America's side is winning, but he becomes disillusioned by the violence and lack of public support. He surrenders in the hope it will end the war.

Goliath (Dr. Bill Foster) is brutally killed by Ragnarok, a berserk clone of Thor created by Reed Richards. Sue Richards is so furious, she leaves Reed and joins Cap's team.

DASTARDLY DEED!

PROMOTED!
The U.S. president installs victorious Tony Stark as director of S.H.I.E.L.D., and the 50-State Initiative is born.

...ARE YOU ON?

HULK'S REVENGE

- He defeats King of the Inhumans **Black Bolt** on the **moon**

- He builds an arena in the wreckage of **New York City** and forces **Iron Man** and **Mister Fantastic** to **fight** each other!

- **Doctor Strange** is winning, until Hulk crushes his hands to prevent him casting spells

BIG HITTER!

Hulk defeats the Illuminati, but doesn't count on the intervention of the **most powerful hero on Earth!** The mentally unstable **Sentry** sees Hulk's rampage on TV, and decides to unleash his **incredible powers** on the Green Goliath!

TELL ME MORE!

Hulk's ship crash-lands on the planet Sakaar. Its ruler, the Red King, forces Hulk to fight as a gladiator, but the Green Goliath teams up with his fellow gladiators and overthrows him. Hulk becomes Sakaar's ruler and marries Caiera, the Red King's lieutenant. All is well until the ship Hulk arrived on explodes. Caiera is killed and much of Sakaar is destroyed. Hulk blames the Illuminati and invades Earth.

Q: Who are the Illuminati?

A: Formed by Iron Man to respond to **planetary threats**, they are a group of some of Earth's most **powerful** and **brainy** heroes. It includes Iron Man, Black Bolt, Doctor Strange, Mister Fantastic, and Professor X. Only the first four members are involved in **the Hulk's exile.**

THIS MEANS WAR!

The Illuminati mean well when they arrange for the **troublesome Hulk** to be **marooned in outer space.** But Hulk **makes it back** to Earth and, thirsting for **revenge**, declares **World War Hulk!**

DISASTER AREA!

Hulk's ally **Miek** reveals that he knew the **Red King** had rigged Hulk's **ship to explode,** but didn't tell him. Miek causes **thousands of deaths** just to trick Hulk into fighting again!

THE WAR IS OVER
Hulk finally realises that he's just got **too angry** and asks Iron Man to stop him. **Satellites** blast Hulk, **knocking him out.** As Bruce Banner, he is captured and imprisoned **six miles** underground.

WOW!
139,000
The number of workers needed to fix up New York City after Hulk and his friends' rampage!

TEAM PLAYERS
To invade **Earth,** Hulk recruits **fellow Earth,** his **Warbound** from Sakaar **the gladiators** (Arch-E-5912, No-Name of the Brood, Korg, Miek the Hiroim, and Mung).

NOooooo!!
The U.S. Army and almost all of Earth's heroes try to **STOP THE HULK.** Their battleground, New York City, is left in **RUINS** and thousands of people are put in danger.

To defeat Ultron, Wolverine and the Invisible Woman go back in time to kill Hank Pym, stopping him from creating Ultron Mark I. When they return to the present, the world has changed – and not for the better! The Avengers have disbanded, a cyborg Tony Stark governs and the heroes of Earth fight the dark magic of Morgan Le Fay instead of evil robots!

REALLY?!

Ultron doesn't take the risk of **confronting the surviving heroes** himself – he runs his Age of Destruction **from the future!** Vision **acts as his slave** and commands the empire.

TOP 3

Ways to Defeat Ultron

1 PERSUADE Hank Pym not to create Ultron

2 KILL Hank Pym before he can create Ultron

3 INFECT Ultron with a computer virus

NOOOOO!! Wolverine and the Invisible Woman's time-travelling causes a huge rip in SPACE AND TIME, triggering the COLLAPSE of the MULTIVERSE!

Hank Pym gets a lot of flack for creating Ultron, but if you ask the original Ant-Man himself, he would claim he just created Ultron Mark I. The genius android then upgraded itself, creating the evil Ultron.

WOW!

6,978

The number of heroes Ultron takes out – from 7,000 to only 22!

BAD DAY

The **Savage Land** might seem like a **pretty safe place** to park your **flying car,** but a **young Nick Fury** gets a shock when he finds his has been **stolen** – by a **time-travelling Wolverine!**

AAARRGHH!!

When **LUKE CAGE** and **SHE-HULK** try to infiltrate **ULTRON'S FORTRESS,** they fail, but reveal Ultron's **BIG SECRET** – he is ruling the world **FROM THE FUTURE!**

S.H.I.E.L.D. DECLASSIFIED

DISASTER AVERTED
When killing Hank Pym creates an even worse future, the Invisible Woman and Wolverine go back in time again. They convince Hank to fit a shut-down mechanism in Ultron. When the mad mechanoid launches his attack, Iron Man triggers the hidden programme, averting the Age of Ultron.

RISE OF THE ROBOTS!

The Age of Ultron has begun! The evil sentient robot **conquers Earth** and rules with an **Adamantium fist.** The few Super Heroes who remain must travel **back through time** to save the world from a **devastating future!**

227

ALTERNATE
WORLDS

BLAST FROM THE PAST

TELL ME MORE!

INTRUDERS IN TIME!
Steve Rogers is banished to the past by the wicked Purple Man. Rogers' presence in 1602 creates a hole in the fabric of reality, which could potentially lead to the destruction of the world. It also makes superhumans appear centuries too early!

Sir Richard Reed

Dr Stephen Strange

Matthew Murdoch

Carlos Javier

Peter Parquagh

Virginia Dare

Strange, ominous storms are sweeping Britain and Europe – it seems that the **end of the world** is nigh! In the **reality of 1602** live some familiar Super Heroes and Super Villains... but with a **unique, Elizabethan twist!**

BACK FROM THE DEAD!

James I **executes** Dr Strange for witchcraft – but his sweetheart, Lady Clea, retrieves his **severed head**, which can still **communicate** through **magical means!**

TOP V.I.P.s OF THE 1602 REALITY

KING JAMES I OF ENGLAND AND VI OF SCOTLAND
James hates witches and cuts a deal with Magnus to get rid of Witchbreed (mutants), too!

VIRGINIA DARE
The first person born in the English New World colonies. She can transform into any creature, including dinosaurs and mythical beasts!

WILLIAM SHAKESPEARE
The Bard is kidnapped and made to chronicle the adventures of Otto Von Doom!

QUEEN ELIZABETH I
Good Queen Bess is assassinated by agents of evil Count Otto Von Doom!

Rojhaz

Sir Nicholas Fury

BETWEEN...

1602 covers artist Scott McKowen recreated the look of historical engravings with a technique named "scratchboard" – scratching through a layer of ink to a hard chalk surface. He added scrolls and flags for extra period feel.

...THE PANELS

DASTARDLY DEED!

Spanish Inquisition leader **Enrique Magnus** tracks down mutant **Witchbreed** and **burns** them at the **stake**. Enrique, secretly a Witchbreed himself, is obsessed with hunting **Master Javier** – head of a **school** that shelters Witchbreed.

YEGGH!

Baron Octavius is an evil Italian aristocrat suffering from the plague. He injects himself with octopus blood as a cure, but turns into a weird half-octopus creature!

TOP 12 Familiar Faces

1. **DOCTOR STEPHEN STRANGE** – Queen Elizabeth's physician and a secret magician (Doctor Strange)

2. **MASTER CARLOS JAVIER** – of Javier's Select College for the Sons of Gentlefolk (Professor X)

3. **SIR NICHOLAS FURY** – Elizabeth's spymaster (Nick Fury Sr)

4. **GRAND INQUISITOR ENRIQUE MAGNUS** – of the Spanish Inquisition (Magneto)

5. **DONAL** – ancient member of the Knights Templar (Thor)

6. **PETER PARQUAGH** – Nicholas Fury's assistant (Peter Parker)

7. **THE FOUR OF THE SHIP FANTASTICK** – a team of explorers (Fantastic Four)

8. **COUNT OTTO VON DOOM** – of Latveria (Doctor Doom)

9. **MASTER DAVID BANNER** – ruthless agent of King James I (Incredible Hulk)

10. **LORD IRON** – a Spanish inventor imprisoned by David Banner (Iron Man)

11. **ROJHAZ** – a mysterious Native American (Captain America)

12. **MATTHEW MURDOCH** – a mercenary, posing as a blind minstrel (Daredevil)

ARTIFICIAL ASGARDIANS!
The Alchemax Corporation creates its own Norse heroes, the Aesir, and claims that they are the real Thor, Hela, Heimdall, Baldur and Loki. They even build a floating city called Valhalla...

TOP 5 WAYS TO BECOME A SUPER HERO IN 2099

GET YOUR GENES TWEAKED by a sabotaged genetic experiment like Spider-Man (Miguel O'Hara).

GET YOUR CONSCIOUSNESS UPLOADED into a robot body like Ghost Rider (Kenshiro "Zero" Cochrane).

GET MUTATED by radiation and gain the ability to shoot bio-energy like Ravage (Paul-Phillip Ravage).

GET BLASTED with a powerful gamma-radiation weapon like the Hulk (John Eisenhart).

GET BRAINWASHED into believing you're a Norse God like Thor (Cecil McAdam).

Power Up!

SPIDER HAMMER
What's better than having spider-powers? Having spider-powers and **THOR'S MAGICAL HAMMER!** When **STEVE ROGERS** (Captain America) throws **MJOLNIR** to **SPIDER-MAN**, the web-slinger proves that he is **WORTHY TO WIELD** the mighty weapon!

WHAT?!

In 2099, two heroes are **worshipped** by **fanatical cults!** The **Knights of Banner** worship the Hulk, and the **Thorites** worship Thor. (They even dress in Thor **costumes** while flying around on **hang-gliders** and swinging **big hammers**...)

YECCH!

The Earth of 2099 is horrible, but Hellrock island makes the rest of it look like paradise! Hellrock is polluted with radioactive waste and inhabited by prisoners who have turned into gruesome "Mutroids".

TOP 5 — 2099 Must-Haves!

1. **A HOLOGRAPHIC COMPUTERISED PERSONAL ASSISTANT** – such as Miguel O'Hara's "virtual secretary", Lyla.

2. **A HOVER-CAR** – wheels are so last century!

3. **A CARD IMPLANT** – no more real money! Store your virtual cash in a "card" implanted under your skin!

4. **A MICROWAVE GUN** – why shoot your enemies when you can cook them?

5. **A PLATE OF SYNTH-FOOD** – 100% cheap 'n' tasty chemicals. Yum!

WANT TO KNOW THE FUTURE?

Welcome to a **grim** and **gritty future!** In **2099**, **megacorporations** run everything and ordinary people **struggle to survive.** Thankfully, a **new generation** of heroes emerges to fight for justice – but the bad guys are **never far behind...**

1,288

The top speed of the Punisher's H.D. Stealth Stinger in kph (800mph). This police motorcycle can also become invisible and turn traffic lights to green!

GOOD DAY

The Doctor Doom of 2099 is not content with ruling his **tiny kingdom**, Latveria – he also **conquers** the U.S.A. and declares himself **president!**

BETWEEN...

Starting with Doom 2099 #29 (May 1995), all 2099 comics had the letters "AD" added to their title. The letters stand for "Anno Doom", (the year of Doom) to indicate Doom has taken over!

...THE PANELS

Nooooo!! Invading **PHALANX ALIENS** melt the polar ice caps and raise sea levels. **NEW YORK** is **FLOODED** and then attacked by **ATLANTEANS!**

EXPECT THE UNEXPECTED!

There are other realities **beyond Earth-616** – realities where everything is **upside down,** where history has taken **wildly different paths.** That's when things can get **really, really weird!**

HULK

BRUCE BANNER

YECCH!

In one grim future, Hulk is the last person alive after a nuclear war. Each day he's eaten by swarms of bugs – but his healing factor restores him to be devoured again and again...

SPIDER-STAR!
On Earth-80219, Spider-Man **stops** the burglar that kills Uncle Ben (on our Earth-616) and **doesn't become** a crime fighter. Instead, he exploits his amazing powers as **a star of action movies.** Peter Parker still has to learn that "with great power comes **great responsibility**"!

RICK SMASH!
On Earth-7812, **RICK JONES** becomes the Hulk – and does an **EXCELLENT JOB!** As Hulk, he joins the Avengers, becomes Captain America's new sidekick, ends the Kree/Skrull war and punches Annihilus **IN THE FACE!**

Power Up!

TELL ME MORE!

In the Mangaverse (Earth-2301), Toni Stark is the armour-clad Iron Maiden, Peter Parker is a ninja of the Spider-Clan who has sworn to avenge his uncle and Hank Pym is a kid genius and rock star!

AUNTIE HERO!
Why should Peter Parker have all the fun? **Aunt May** becomes a superhuman senior citizen as the armoured **Golden Oldie** on Earth-24388, shrinking **Ant-Aunt** on Earth-23848 and the chilling **Auntie-Freeze** on Earth-24838!

WHEN BAD GUYS GO GOO

X-RATED!
In the Mutant X Universe (Earth-1298), the villain Magneto is a hero! Professor X and the X-Men are villains and S.H.I.E.L.D. is a terrorist group.

TOP 6

Grim Alternate Realities

1
DAYS OF FUTURE PAST – mutant-hunting Sentinels try to take over the world!

2
AGE OF APOCALYPSE (EARTH-295) – Professor X is killed, leading to a horrible future where Apocalypse rules!

3
EARTH-81727 – Jean Grey does not sacrifice herself to destroy the Dark Phoenix and it destroys the universe!

4
ZOMBIVERSE (EARTH-2149) – heroes are infected with a zombie virus, eat everyone in their world and seek more universes to devour!

5
AGE OF ULTRON (EARTH-61112) – Ultron rules and is trying to exterminate humanity!

6
CROOKED WORLD (EARTH-238) – Captain Britain gets trapped in this weird world ruled by the reality-warping mutant Mad Jim Jaspers.

WHEN GOOD GUYS GO BA

BAD BEAST
Beast (Hank McCoy) is one of the most heroic X-Men, but in the alternate future of the Age of Apocalypse, Hank's famous for being cruel! He works as a genetic engineer, performing experiments on mutant prisoners.

MAD JIM JASPER

WOW!

3007

The year the Guardians of the Galaxy are founded in the alternate future of Earth-691.

WAR OF THE WORLDS
Martians invade **freedom-fighter Killraven's reality** (Earth-691). These octopoid oppressors don't just want land – they want to **exploit humanity as food!**

INDEX

8-Ball 92
50-State Initiative 139, 147, 199, 222–3,

A

Aarkus 197
Aaronson, Adam 205
A-Bomb 44, 110, 111
Abomination 44, 98–9, 110
Absorbing Man 112, 113, 167
A-Force 32, 221
Agamotto the All-Seeing 15, 59
Age of Ultron 226–7, 235
Agent 13 11, 158, 222
Agent Venom 77
Agents of Atlas 174–5
Aggamon the All-Powerful 184
A.I.M. 11, 31, 73, 91, 154, 165, 200–1, 213
Albion 87
Alchemax Corporation 232
Alkhema 194–5
All-Mother 181
Alpha Flight 12, 32, 146–7, 188
Amatsu-Kami 151
Amatsu-Mikaboshi 15, 150, 185
Amora 180
Ancient One 58, 80, 86
Angel 130–1, 139
Angela 181
Annex 199
Annihilus 234
Ant-Man 20–1, 24–5, 47, 90, 126–7 see
   also Pym, Hank; Lang, Scott
Anti-Venom 77
Apocalypse 14, 99, 130–1, 150, 221, 235
Apocalypse Beast 94
Apocalypse Twins 71
Arcade 142–3, 204
Arm'Chedon 173
Armadillo 91
Arrow 26
Asgard 28–31, 40, 68–9, 75, 87, 100–1,
   112, 117, 150–1, 180–3, 184, 210–11
Asmodeus 58
Astro, Vance 136
Atlantis 12–13, 114–15, 187
Atlas 83, 171
Atlas Foundation 174–5
Attilan 134, 187
Attuma 12, 114–15
Atum the God Eater 151
Aurora 146–7
Avengers 11, 18, 21, 22–3, 25, 26–7, 35,
   39, 45, 46–7, 53, 54, 58, 67, 68, 70, 71, 72,
   74, 77, 83, 87, 98, 101, 106, 124–5, 126–7,
   128–9, 141, 154, 156–7, 164, 166–7,
   170–1, 194, 195, 197, 198–9, 202
Avengers Academy 126–7, 129, 143
Avengers A.I. 20, 205
Avenging Son 12
Awesome Android 90, 201
Awesome Andy 210
Axis 156

B

Badoon 137, 173
Bagalia 142, 166, 186
Banner, Dr Bruce 44–5, 98–9, 113, 115,
   188, 201, 225, 234
Banner, Master David 231
Bardas, Lucia von 157
Barnes, Bucky 10, 11, 35, 83, 208
Baron Blood 59, 141
Baroness 83
Barton, Barney 26
Basilisk 92–3
Bast 15
Batroc 170
Battleworld 14, 77, 112, 161, 209, 220–1
Baxter Building 132–3, 187
Beast 13, 130–1, 139, 235
Beetle 91
Ben, Uncle 52, 119, 234
Bessie the Vampire Cow 59
Beta Ray Bill 40, 210–11
Beyonder 14, 112
Beyonders 208, 209, 220
Bi-Beast 63
Big Bertha 129
Big Wheel 91
Binary 32–3
Black Bolt 13, 135, 224
Black Cat 53
Blackheart 60, 175
Black King 174, 175
Black Knight 126, 140–1, 166
Black Panther 13, 36–7, 88, 126, 155, 188,
   208
Black Racer 49
Black Talon 170
Black Widow 26, 27, 34–5, 39, 55, 126,
   128, 159
Blade 60, 140
Blake, Donald 31, 211
Blazing Skull 139
Blizzard 19
Bloodstone, Elsa 149
Bloodstone, Ulysses 213
Bogeyman 145
Braddock, Brian 141
Brainstorm 111
Brood 161, 172–3, 225
Brotherhood of Evil Mutants 46, 130
Brotherhood of the Shield 161
Bruiser 117
Builders 173
Bulldozer 167
Bullfrog 62
Bullseye 39, 84, 109
Buried Alien 48, 49
Buzzard 62

C

Cabal 220–1
Cage, Luke 39, 113, 119, 138, 201, 227
Cagliostro 215

Caiera 224
Calypso 87
Captain America 8–11, 12, 26, 27, 30, 33,
   35, 70, 72, 74, 82–3, 91, 106–7, 119,
   126–7, 129, 161, 166, 201, 222–3, 231, 232
Captain America's Shield 11, 70, 208–9
Captain Britain 26, 87, 140–1, 235
Captain Marvel 22, 32–3, 49, 117, 147
Captain Mar-Vell 66
Captain Midlands 141
Captain Uni-Mutt 41
Captain Universe 41
Caretaker 60
Carnage 76, 77
Carrion 88–9
Carter, Sharon 11, 72, 158, 161
Cat 119
Cavalry 158
Celestials 80, 150, 151, 161
Chameleon 91, 169
Champions of Los Angeles 34
Champion of the Universe 113
Chang, Monica 20
Chaos War 150
Charlie-27 136
Chewie 32–3
Children of Tomorrow 126
Chitauri 172–3
Cho, Amadeus 110, 189
Chondu the Mystic 87
Chthon 15, 46–7
Clea 58, 80–1
Clea, Lady 230
Cloak and Dagger 143
Collector 41
Colossus 117, 130, 139
Constrictor 91
Cooper, Carlie 105
Cosmic Cube 66, 73, 106, 161, 200–1, 213
Coulson, Phillip 128, 157, 158–9
Counterweight 145
Creel, Crusher 112
Crimson Cosmos 185
Crimson Cowl 167, 195
Crimson Dynamo 19
Crossbones 72, 73, 222
Crossfire 27
Crystal 134–5
cyborgs 34, 147, 194, 204–5
Cyborg-Sinister 200
Cyclops 130–1
Cyttorak 15, 116, 185

D

da Vinci, Leonardo 159, 161
de Fontaine, Contessa 159
Daken 148
Daredevil 34, 38–9, 53, 108–9, 118, 231
   see also Murdock, Matt
Dark Avengers 26, 74–5, 128–9, 181
Dark Dimension 80–1, 184–5
Dark Elves 180
Dark Phoenix 235

Daywalkers 60
Deadpool 178
DeAngelo, Devlin 201
Death 14, 15, 66–7, 212
Deathbird 33
Death-Dealer 203
Death Locket 204–5
Deathlok 158, 204–5
Death Spore 164
Defenders 58, 61, 138–9
Demogorge 151
Destroyer 68, 151
Deviants 95
Devil Dinosaur 63, 188–9
Diamondback 91
Digitek 141
Dimitrios 20
Dinah Soar 129
Dire Wraith 87, 178
Ditko, Steve 59
Doc Green 45
Doc Samson 45, 110
Doctor Bong 92
Doctor Doom 25, 33, 46–7, 61, 63, 71, 83,
   86, 112, 132–3, 156, 194, 205, 208, 209,
   220–1, 231
Doctor Dorcas 114
Doctor Faustus 11, 72, 91
Doctor Octopus (Doc Ock) 52, 53, 54, 70,
   78–9, 167, 168–9, 231
Doctor Strange 15, 56–9, 69, 80–1, 86–7,
   138–9, 148, 174, 184–5, 214–15, 221, 224,
   230–1
Doctor Voodoo 60, 214
Domain of Apocalypse 221
Doombots 20, 166, 205
Doom the Living Planet 178
Doomsday Robot 205
Doorman 129
Dormammu 46, 58, 80–1, 86, 184–5
Douglas, Arthur 136
Dracula 60–1, 140–1
Drax the Destroyer 66–7, 136–7
Dreamstalker 61
Drew, Jessica 54–5
Drew, Jonathan 55
Drew, Miriam 55
Dum Dum Dugan 156–7, 158–9, 160
Duval, Paul 88

E

Ebony Blade 140, 214
Egghead 20–1, 22, 90–1, 138, 167
Ego the Living Planet 40, 178–9
Elder Gods 86
Electro 39, 53, 79, 95, 168–9
Elektra 38, 84, 109, 118–19
Emissaries of Evil 138
Enchantress 30, 87, 180
Energizer 144–5
Eon 41
Erskine, Dr. 10, 11
Eternals 179, 187

Eternity 14, 80–1, 214
Everett, Bill 12
Excalibur 140, 141
Executioner 87, 180
Extremis 19, 103
Eye of Agamotto 214

F

Fafnir 180
Falcon 10, 11, 126, 128, 208
Falsworth, Lady Jacqueline 49, 141
Faltines 80–1, 185
Fandral the Dashing 30
Fang, General 45
Fantastic Four 12, 25, 37, 53, 70, 79, 82, 90, 94, 115, 116, 126, 130, 132–3, 164, 173, 202, 213
Fearless Defenders 139
Femme Force 158
Fenris Wolf 180
Fin Fang Foom 63, 95, 102, 111, 202–3
Fin Fang Four 95
Firestar 53
Fitz, Leo 158
Flatman 129
Force Works 47
Foster, Dr Bill 223
Foster, Jane 31, 68, 117, 211
Four Horsemen of Death 71
FrankenCastle 148
Franklin, Mattie 54
Frightful Four 132, 134
Frost, Emma 130, 175
Frost Giants 69, 180
Fury, Jake 157, 165
Fury, Max 155
Fury, Mikal 157
Fury, Nick 10, 11, 54, 82, 126, 155, 156–7, 158–9, 160–1, 164–5, 227
Fury, Nick, Jr. 126, 128, 156–7, 158
Fury, Sir Nicholas 231
Future Foundation 134, 144, 168

G

Gaea 15, 81
Galactus 59, 63, 161, 178–9, 213
Gamma Flight 147
Gamora 66, 136–7
Gargoyle 139
Garokk 188
Gatherers 126
Geiger 199
Genosha 186
Gerber, Steve 86
Gertrude 143
Ghost Riders 60–1, 139, 149, 232
Giant Man 20–1
Gibborim 142
Giganto 12
Gingerbread Man 59
Goblin Formula 74–5, 104–5
Goblin King 74–5
Godforce 211
Godkiller 151, 214
Gods of Heliopolis 151
Golden Avenger 16
Golden Oldie 234
Goliath 20–1, 26, 166–7, 170, 223
Gomdulla 95
Goodman, Martin 113
Googam 95

Goom 95
Gorgilla 95
Gorgolla 92
Gorgon 164
Gorilla-Man 175
Grandmaster 15
Graviton 88
Great Beasts 147
Great Lakes Avengers 63, 128–9
Green, Dorothy 59
Green Giant 99
Green Goblin 25, 53, 74–5, 104–5, 168 see also Osborn, Norman
Grey, Jean 15, 130–1, 235
Grey Gargoyle 88
Grey Goblin 105
Grim Reaper 91, 170–1
Grizzly 25
Groot 95, 137
Grottu 95
Guardian 146–7
Guardians of the Galaxy 32, 67, 77, 136–7, 167

H

Hades 184
Hairball 128
Hala 179
Halfworld 137, 178
Hall, Franklin 88
Hamilton, Bart 105
H.A.M.M.E.R. 74–5, 155, 170
Hammer, Justin 85, 99
Hammer, Justine 167
Hammerhead 85
Hand, The 35, 38, 119, 165, 174–5
Hands of the Dead 214
Hansen, Maya 103
Harkness, Agatha 46, 132
Hawkeye 23, 26–7, 34, 35, 55, 126, 128, 129
Hayes, Henry 158, 205
Hayes, Molly 117, 142–3
H.D. Stealth Stinger 233
Headmen 92, 138
Heavy Metal 201
Heimdall 180–1
Hel 150, 184
Hela 100, 150, 180, 184–5
Heli 180
Hellfire Club 174–5
Hellrock 232
Hellsgaard, Robert 149
Hell's Kitchen 108, 187
Hellstrom, Daiman 60–1, 214
Hercules 116–17, 126, 150–1, 185
Heroes for Hire 119
High Evolutionary 40, 46, 178, 198
Hill, Maria 155, 159
Hillman, Terrence 39
Hiroim 225
Hiro-Kala 98
Hit Monkey 160
Hive 165
Hobgoblin 91, 105, 168
Hogun the Grim 30
Hogzilla 62
Hollister, Lily 105
Hood, The 85
Horn of Proteus 12
Horsemen of Apocalypse 99

Howard the Duck 59
Howling Commandos 82, 156–7, 159, 160
Ho Yinsen 18
Hudson, James 146
Hulk 31, 42–5, 53, 59, 80, 91, 98–9, 100, 110, 115, 116, 126–7, 137, 138–9, 169, 173, 201, 202, 212, 221, 224–5, 231, 232, 234
Hulkbusters 17, 19, 45, 87, 98, 116
Human Torch 12, 24, 26, 49, 53, 132–3, 134, 197
Hunter of Monster Special Forces 149
Hussain, Faiza 140
Hydra 11, 35, 54–5, 72, 83, 91, 154, 156, 157, 159, 161, 164–5, 223
Hydro 17, 19

I

Iceman 130–1, 139
Id the Selfish Moon 178
Idunn 30
Illuminati 99, 213, 224–5
Immortus 71
Imperius Rex 12–13
Impossible Man 39, 178
In-Betweener 14
Infinity Formula 156–7
Infinity Gauntlet 66, 208, 212
Infinity Gems 66–7, 113, 212–13
Inhumans 134–5, 173
Intelligencia 110
Invader 82
Invisible Woman 12, 14, 132–3, 223, 226–7
Iron Destroyer 17, 19
Iron Fist 15, 39, 44, 118–19, 138
Iron Fists 187
Iron Lad 47, 70
Iron Man 13, 16–19, 27, 34, 35, 74, 86, 98, 99, 102–3, 126–7, 137, 148, 155, 160, 195, 203, 224, 231 see also Stark, Tony
Iron Nail 10
Iron Patriot 18, 74, 129
It 95

J

Jackal 53, 89, 90–1
Jack Hammer 145
Jack of Hearts 126
Jakes, Judson 137
Jameson, J. Jonah 53, 91
Jarella 45
Jarvis, Edwin 126–7, 194
Jason of Spartax 137
Jaxon, Jerome 147
Jocasta 194–5, 198–9, 202–3
Joe Fixit 45
Johnson, Daisy 156, 158
Johnson, Marcus 157
Jones, Gabe 157
Jones, Jessica 201
Jones, Nia 158
Jones, Rick 44, 110, 116, 126, 234
Jotunheim 180
J'son 137
Juggernaut 15, 116, 130–1, 148
Juniper, Jonathan 157

K

Kaifi, Elloe 225
Kaine 78
Kang the Conqueror 21, 70–1, 126–7

Karkas 92
Karnak 118
Karolina 143
Kawasaki, Wendy 147
Ka-Zar 86, 128, 188–9
Khan, Kamala 33, 135
Kid Immortus 70
Kid Loki 68
Killmonger 37
Killpower 141
Killraven 235
Kinder 83
Kingpig 62
Kingpin 39, 53, 84–5, 108–9
Kirby, Jack 37, 113, 157, 165, 203
Klaw 88, 132
Klaw, Ulysses 36, 37
Kluh 99
Klyntar 76
Knights of Banner 232
Knights of Pendragon 87
Knowwhere 40
Korg 225
Korvac, Michael 204–5
Kraken 164, 165
Krakoa the Living Island 186
Kraven the Hunter 79, 87, 168–9
Kree 15, 26, 27, 32–3, 66, 83, 135, 136, 172–3, 179, 213
Kubrick, Jack 202
K'un-Lun 187
Kurse 145
Kuurth 148
Kyln 178
Kymellians 173

L

Lady Dorma 115
Lady Liberators 87
Lady Loki 68
Lady Sif 180
Lady Spider 169
Lang, Cassandra 24–5, 70
Lang, Scott 24–5, 126 see also Ant-Man
Last Defenders 139
Latveria 33
Le Fay, Caroline 139
Le Fay, Morgan 15, 21, 54, 55, 86, 226
Leader, The 44, 91, 99, 110, 212
Leapfrog 142–3
Lee, Stan 18, 31, 37, 39, 52, 53, 81, 113, 127, 133, 157, 165
Legion of Monsters 148–9
Lethal Legion 170–1
Leviathan 157
Life Model Decoys (LMDs) 154–5, 159
Lightmaster 167
Lightspeed 144–5
Limbo 145, 173, 185
Lionheart 141
Lipton, Alex 197
Living Laser 88–9, 91, 170
Living Tribunal 14
Lizard 79, 88–9
Lhasa 45
Lockheed 128
Lockjaw 128, 135
Loki 30, 45, 68–9, 80, 100–1, 126, 139, 150, 180–1, 214–15
Lord Chaos 14
Lucky 26

Lukin, Aleksander 73
Lyla 232
Lyra 111

M

M-11 175, 204
M-13 140–1
McAdam, Cecil 232
McBride, Malcolm 88
Machine Man 198–9, 201, 202–3
Machine Sentinel 202–3
Machinesmith 107, 204
Machine Teen 204–5
Macho, Count 59
McKowen, Scott 231
MacLain, Dr Myron 208
Madame Hydra 121, 159, 160, 164
Madame Masque 85
Madame Menace 202–3
Madame Web 54
Mad Jim Jaspers 235
Mad Merlin 87
Mad Thinker 90–1
Maestro 45, 221
Maggia 85
Magic Pig 117
Magik 130
Magneto 46, 47, 70, 130, 209, 235
Magnus, Enrique 231
Magnus, Will 199
Magus 137
Maker 220–1
Makkari 48–9
Maklu 102
Malekith 30, 214
Malus, Dr Karl 90–1
Man-Ape 37, 170
Mancha, Victor 20, 142–3, 194, 204–5
Mandarin 91, 102–3, 205
Mandaringtail 103
Manelli, Dino 157
Manidoog 151
Manning, Luther 205
Manphibian 149
Man-Thing 59, 63, 86, 119, 148–9, 160, 189
Marrina 146–7
Martinex 136
Marvel Boy 175
Marvel Girl 131
Mar-Vell 32–3
Mary Jane 52–3, 104
Mass Master 144–5
Master of All Reality 200
Master of Evil 25, 127
Master Javier 231
Master of the Mystic Arts 58
Master Order 14
Master Pandemonium 46, 60
Master Planner 79
Master of the World 147
Masters, Alicia 132–3
Masters of Evil 20, 61, 79, 82, 83, 91, 126, 154, 166–7, 194–5
Masterson, Eric 211
Masterson, Kevin 100
Maximoff, Pietro 46, 49
Maximoff, Wanda 46–7, 197
Maximus the Mad 91, 135
May, Aunt 52, 53, 79, 84, 128, 214, 234
May, Melinda 158

Medusa 134–5
Meggan 141
Mentallo 91, 161
Mephisto 46, 53, 175
Merlin 87, 141, 214
Merlyn 87
Midgard Serpent 116
Midnight Wreckers 203
Miek 225
Mighty Avengers 21
Mimic 201
Mind Gem 128
Mindless Ones 80, 81
Minoru, Nico 142–3, 214
Mister Fantastic 12, 13, 14, 18, 71, 76, 132–3, 144, 161, 200, 220-1, 222, 223, 224
Mister Hyde 90–1, 127, 166
Mister Immortal 129
Mister Knife 179
Mister Negative 77, 85
Mister Sinister 131
Mistress of Destiny 145
Misty Knight 139
Mjolnir 28–31, 68–9, 70, 101, 180–1, 210–11, 232
M'Kraan Crystal 179
Mockingbird 27, 129, 158
M.O.D.O.K. 55, 63, 90–1, 92–3, 110, 128, 159
Mojo 92, 137, 169
Molecula 145
Molecule Man 45, 208, 220
Mole Man 132
Molten Man 88–9
Monkey Joe 129
Monster Isle 94, 186
Monster Metropolis 148–9
Moon Boy 59, 63, 188–9
Moondragon 66, 138–9
Moon Knight 148
Moonstone 33, 83, 166
Morbius 90–1, 148, 149
Mordo, Baron 58, 81, 86
Motormouth 141
Ms Lion 128
Ms Marvel 32–3, 117, 135, 147
Muir Island 186
Mulligan, Pat 77
Mung 225
Muramasa Blade 214
Murderworld 204
Murdock, Matt 34, 38–9, 108–9, 230-1 see also Daredevil
Muspelheim 180
Mutant X Universe 235
Mutroids 232
Mys-Tech 141
Mysterio 79, 91, 168–9
Mystique 131

N

Namor the Sub-Mariner 12–13, 37, 114–15, 138–9, 187, 224
Nebula 66, 204
Nebulon 138
Needle 92–3
Nefaria, Count 85, 170–1
Nekra 171
Nelson, Foggy 39, 109
Nelvanna 147
Nerkkod 115

New Avengers 55
New Defenders 139
New Mutants 130
Newton, Isaac 161
New Warriors 49, 62, 223
Nextwave 80, 202
Nidavellir 180
Nightcrawler 130
Nighthawk 87, 138–9
Nightmare 58, 60–1, 184–5
Nightmask 204
Nightshade 10, 91
Night Shift 93
Nitro the Living Bomb 12, 49, 223
N'Kantu 148–9
Noll, Criti 22
Nomad 10
No-Name 225
Northstar 146–7
Nova 213
Nova Helmet 213
Nova Prime 40
Nuke 84
Nuwali 187, 189

O

Oberon of Otherworld 141
Oblivion 14
Octavius, Baron Victor 231
Odin 40, 68–9, 101, 150, 180–1, 210–11
Odinsword 214
O'Grady, Eric 25
O'Hara, Miguel 232
Old Lace 143
Old Man Logan 130
Olson, Jake 31
Olympia 187
Olympus Group 184
Omega Flight 147
One-Above-All 14
Orb 92
Orion 157
Osborn, Harry 75, 89, 104–5
Osborn, Norman 12, 19, 25, 53, 74–5, 83, 100, 104–5, 128, 129, 155, 170, 181, 222 see also Green Goblin
Oshtur the Omnipotent 15, 59

P

Page, Karen 39, 109
Parker, Peter 39, 52–3, 55, 75, 78–9, 84, 89, 104–5, 119, 149, 222, 234 see also Spider-Man
Parks, Arthur 88
Parquagh, Peter 230
Pet Avengers 59, 128
Petrovich, Ivan 34
Phalanx 136, 194–5, 233
Phoenix 15
Phoenix Force 13, 15, 47
Photon 202
Phyla-Vell 200
Piledriver 167
Plodex 146
Plokta 81, 141
Plunder, Kevin 188
Pluto 117, 150, 184–5
Porcupine 170
Porker, Peter 76
Pork Grind 76
Potts, Pepper 19

Power, Dr James 144–5
Power, Margaret 144
Power Man 44, 126, 171
Power Pack 144–5
Powerpax 145
Power Prism 22
Prast, Klara 142–3
Princess Powerful 117
Professor X 72, 130, 224, 235
Project 42 222
Protectors of the Universe 41
Proteus 14
Pryde, Kitty 128, 130
Puck 146–7
Puma 91
Punisher, The 148, 233
Puppet Master 132
Purple Man 230
Pym, Hank 20–1, 22–3, 24, 126–7, 129, 164, 167, 170, 194–5, 196, 205, 222, 226–7, 234 see also Ant-Man

Q

Quake 158
Quantum Bands 41, 213
Quasar 126
Queen of Angels 181
Quicksilver 46, 48–9, 126, 134
Quill, Peter 137

R

Ragnarok 30, 68, 180–1, 223
Rakasha 60
Ralston, Rebel 157
Rand, Daniel 118
Rappaccini, Monica 91
Rasputin, Piotr 117
Ravage 232
Ravonna Renslayer, Princess 71
Red Ghost 91, 132
Red Guardian 34
Red Hulk 90, 98, 110–11, 126, 188
Red King 44, 224–5
Red Norvell 211
Red Rajah 58
Red She-Hulk 90, 110–11, 138
Red Skull 11, 19, 69, 72–3, 82, 106–7, 156, 160, 213
Redwing 128
Reed, Sir Richard 230
Reilly, Ben 105
Reptil 188
Rescue 19
Reynolds, Bob 117
Rhino 44, 99, 117, 169
Rhodes, Jim 18, 129
Richards, Franklin 12, 14, 27
Richards, Nathaniel 70–1
Rickford, Dave 10
Riggs, Dr Annabelle 139
Rocket Raccoon 48–9, 136–7, 178
Rocket Racer 91
Rogers, Steve 10–11, 12, 128, 158, 208, 230, 232 see also Captain America
Rogue 33
Rorkannu 80
Rose, The 85
Ross, Betty 110–11
Ross, General Thaddeus 111
Runaways 142–3, 214

S

Sabretooth 131
Sakaar 44, 224–5
Sandman 84, 168–9
Sasquatch 146–7
Satana 148–9
Satannish 60–1
Sauron 188
Savage Banner 45
Savage Hulks 221
Savage Land 128, 187, 188–9, 227
Savage She-Hulk 111
Scarlet Centurion 71
Scarlet Spider 105
Scarlet Witch 26, 27, 46–7, 69, 80, 126, 131, 197, 198
Scorpio 157, 160
Scorpion 90
Secret Avengers 25, 26, 55, 128, 154, 157
Secret Defenders 139
Secret Empire 165
Secret Warriors 156, 158, 160, 221
Secret Wars 14, 21, 112, 209
Selene 175
Sentinels 130, 202-3, 235
Sentry 100, 117, 201, 224
Serpent Society 175
Serpent 112, 208
Seth 150
Shadow Council 166–7
Shaman 146–7
Shang-Chi 118, 119, 140
Shanna the She-Devil 86, 188–9
Shark Girl 188
Shaw, Sebastian 174
Shaw, Shinobi 174
She-Hulk 93, 111, 112–13, 126–7, 138–9, 188, 221, 227
Shellhead 98, 103, 116
Shi'ar 33, 173, 179
S.H.I.E.L.D. 11, 19, 35, 54–5, 74, 126, 128, 152–5, 156–7, 158–61, 164, 173, 208, 223
Shuma-Gorath 58
Shuo-Lao the Undying 118
Shuri 36, 37
Silver Centurion 16
Silvermane Manfredi, Silvio 85
Silver Surfer 70, 101, 132, 138–9
Simmons, Jemma 158
Simons, Roscoe 10
Sin 72, 73
Sinister Five 168
Sinister Six 79, 168–9
Sinister Sixty-Six 169
Sinister Twelve 168
Sitwell, Jasper 159
Six Men of Sinestry 169
Skaar 98, 111, 225
Skein 92
Skeleton Crew 106
Skrulls 19, 21, 22, 55, 58, 74, 155, 160, 172–3, 199, 222
Slapstick 62
Sl'gur't 151
Slott, Dan 129
Smasher Goggles 213
Smythe, Alistaire 90, 204
Smythe, Spencer 90–1, 204
Snarks 144–5
Snowbird 146–7

Songbird 83
Sons of Satannish 174
Soria, Adriana 53
Soul Gem 40
Soulsword 214
Space Phantoms 173
Spectrum 126
Speed 47, 48–9
Speedball 49, 128
Speed Demon 48–9
Speedfreek 49
Sphere of Ultimate Knowledge 212
Sphinx 213
Spider Clan 119, 234
Spider-Ham 62, 76, 103
Spider-Hulk 53, 99
Spider-Man 30, 39, 44, 50–3, 55, 59, 74–5, 76, 77, 78–9, 84, 87, 89, 90–1, 104–5, 116, 119, 126–7, 130, 156, 168–9, 214, 222, 232, 234 see also Parker, Peter
Spider-Monkey 52
Spider-Queen 53, 99
Spider-Slayer Robots 204
Spider-Verse 221
Spider-Woman 26, 33, 54–5, 90, 128, 172
Spitfire 49, 140–1
Spot 91
Spymaster 19, 54
Squirrel Girl 59, 63, 129
Stack, Aaron 202–3
Stack, Dr Abel 203
Stacy, Gabriel 75, 105
Stacy, Gwen 75, 104
Stacy, Sarah 75
Stane, Ezekiel 19
Stane, Obadiah 19
Star of Capistan 58
Starfox 66
Stark, Tony 18–19, 30, 34, 88, 102–3, 116, 127, 128, 137, 154–5, 161, 195, 199, 203, 208, 221, 222, 223, 226 see also Iron Man
Starlin, Jim 136
Star-Lord 136–7
Stegron 188–9
Stein, Chase 142–3
Sterns, Samuel 91
Stewart, Alistaire 141
Stick 39, 119
Stilt-Man 39
Stone 35
Stoner, Rick 155
Stones of Norn 215
Storm 37, 130
Storm, Lyja 132
Stormbreaker 40, 210
Stromm, Prof Mendel 74
Strange, Victor 59
Summers, Scott 131
Super-Adaptoid 35, 200–1
superhuman civil war 11, 19, 35, 39, 148, 155, 222–3
Superhuman Registration Act 222–3
Superior Spider-Man 78
Super Sabre 49
Supreme Intelligence 15, 173
Surge 48
Surtur 69, 180–1, 214
Swarm 59, 63
Switzler, Beverly 59
S.W.O.R.D. 55, 154
Swordsman 170

T

Taskmaster 25, 156–7
T'Chaka 36, 37, 88
Teen Abomination 160
Terror 92–3
Thane 66, 135
Thanos 66–7, 126, 135, 136–7, 179, 208, 212
Thing, The 98, 116, 119, 126, 132–3, 221
Thompson, Flash 77
Thor 28–31, 40, 68–9, 70, 87, 100–1, 116–17, 126, 150–1, 180–1, 184, 210–11, 232
Thorr 31
Throg 128, 211
Thunderball 167
Thunderbolts 25, 83, 148, 167, 222
Thunderstrike 100, 211
Tiger Shark 12, 13, 114, 167
Tigra 21, 129
Tim Boo Ba 95
Time Germ 136
Timely, Victor 71
Tink 141
Tinkerer 90–1
Tippy-Toe 63
Titan 179
Titania 112–13, 167
Titano 94–5
Tivan, Taneleer 41
Tombstone 85
Tome of Zhered-Na 215
Toothgnasher 30, 211
Toothgrinder 30
Toxin 77
Trapster 91, 170
Trauma 173
Trickshot 26
Troyjans 173
Turnip Man 59
Typhoid Mary 84, 109

U

Uatu the Watcher 14, 121, 156–7
Ultimate Nullifier 213
Ultimates 32, 157
Ultimo 204–5
Ultra-Adaptoid 91
Ultron 20–1, 70, 126–7, 143, 170, 194–5, 197, 198–9, 202–3, 205, 226–7, 235
Ultron 5 167
Umar 80–1, 185
Uncanny Avengers 128
Uncanny X-Men 130
Union Jack 141
Uni-Power 41
Uranian 175
Urich, Phil 105
U.S. Agent 10

V

Valkyrie 26, 87, 138–9
Vampire by Night 160
Van Dyne, Janet 22–3, 127, 194
Van Dyne, Vernon 23
Venom 26, 76–7, 119
Veranke 55, 74
Vindicator 147
Viper 164–5
Vishanti 15, 59, 215

Vision 20, 46–7, 126–7, 194–5, 196–7, 198
Vodu 151
Void 100, 117
Volstagg the Valiant 30
von Doom, Count Otto 230–1
von Strucker, Baron 35, 82, 156, 160, 164–5
Vulture 53, 79, 168–9

W

Wakanda 13, 15, 36–7, 187, 188–9, 208
War 99
Warbird 33
Warlock 87
Warlock, Adam 40, 67, 136, 137
War Machine 16, 18
Warriors Three 30, 180
Warwolf 160
Wasp 20–1, 22–3, 26, 99, 125, 126–7, 194
Watchers 14, 157, 173, 212
Weatherman 198
Wendigo 147
Werewolf By Night 60, 90, 148–9
West Coast Avengers 21, 128–9, 170
Whiplash 19
Whirlwind 19, 170–1
Whitemane, Aelfyre 144
White Queen 175
White Wolf 37
Whizzer 48, 49
Wiccan 47
Wilder, Alex 142
Wingfoot, Wyatt 132
Winter Soldier 10, 11, 72, 126, 208
Wisdom, Pete 140–1
Witchbreed 231
Wizard 90–1, 132
Wolverine 70, 99, 117, 119, 121, 130–1, 157, 214, 226–7
Wonder Man 46, 117, 127, 129, 170–1, 197
Wong 59, 87
World War Hulk 224–5
Wrecker 116, 166
Wrecking Crew 138

X

Xandu the Mystic 214
Xavin 143
Xemnu 92–3
X-Force 130
Xian 151
X-Men 47, 53, 72, 87, 130–1, 141, 172, 201, 202–3, 235

Y

Yandroth 138–9
Yao 15
Yellowjacket 21, 22, 167
Yondu 136
Yon-Rogg 33
Young Avengers 47, 143

Z

Zabu 128, 188–9
Zemo, Baron 11, 26, 61, 72, 82–3, 91, 126, 160, 164, 166–7
Zeus 15, 150
Zodiac Group 174
Zola, Arnim 72, 73, 92, 160

Senior Editor: Alastair Dougall
Senior Designer: Clive Savage
Project Art Editor: Toby Truphet
Senior Designers: Mark Richards, Anne Sharples
Editors: Ruth Amos, Joel Kempson
Jacket Design: Toby Truphet
Senior Pre-Production Producer: Rebecca Fallowfield
Senior Producer: Alex Bell
Managing Editor: Sadie Smith
Managing Art Editor: Ron Stobbart
Art Director: Lisa Lanzarini
Publisher: Julie Ferris
Publishing Director: Simon Beecroft

Dorling Kindersley would like to thank:
Sarah Brunstad, Brian Overton, Jeff Youngquist
at Marvel for their vital help and advice.
Many thanks also to: Debra Wolter for proofreading;
Cefn Ridout and Allison Singer for editorial assistance;
Kavita Varma, Rosamund Bird, Akansha Jain for design assistance;
Ann Barrett for the index.

First published in Great Britain in 2016 by
Dorling Kindersley Limited
80 Strand, London WC2R 0RL
A Penguin Random House Company

marvel.com

© 2016 MARVEL

Page design copyright © 2016 Dorling Kindersley Limited

10 9 8 7 6 5 4 3 2 1
001-283150-Sept/2016

A CIP catalogue record for this book is
available from the British Library.

ISBN: 978-0-24123-262-0

Printed and bound in China

A WORLD OF IDEAS:
SEE ALL THERE IS TO KNOW

www.dk.com